PLATO'S
SYMPOSIUM
AND **PHAEDRUS**

PLATO'S SYMPOSIUM

AND PHAEDRUS

TRANSLATED BY

JOE SACHS

PAUL DRY BOOKS
Philadelphia 2023

First Paul Dry Books Edition, 2023

Paul Dry Books, Inc.
Philadelphia, Pennsylvania
www.pauldrybooks.com

Printed in the United States of America

Library of Congress Control Number: 2023935578

ISBN 978-1-58988-177-8

Contents

Introduction

TWO OF PLATO'S most popular dialogues have the common topic of love. These dialogues are also both distinctly atypical outings for Socrates. Most Platonic dialogues take place wherever Socrates and others with leisure may bump into each other, or where they agree to meet, in the course of a day in Athens. In both the *Symposium* (174A) and the *Phaedrus* (230D), the reader's attention is called to the unusual circumstances in which Socrates finds himself. He is not normally freshly bathed and groomed and wearing shoes when he gathers with his friends, and he does not normally go outside the city walls, wade in a stream, and lie on the grass to talk with his friends. But in each of these dialogues he accepts an invitation from someone else and falls in with plans not of his own making, plans that differ from his own habits in opposing ways. The *Symposium* is a glittering night-time social event at which some of the most prominent celebrities in Athens deliver speeches, and the *Phaedrus* is an interlude in the middle of a hot day in which one man is seeking a secluded place to memorize a speech.

Just stating these obvious differences reveals one of the most striking similarities between these two dialogues: they entertain us with speeches. And even more than wearing shoes or taking country jaunts, speech-making is contrary to Socrates' preferred mode of spending his time. In the *Gorgias* (461D), he calls it *mak-*

rologia, long-windedness, and says it shows a disregard for the
logos, the rational content of our speech, which he is always urging
those around him to explore and follow.

In the *Symposium*, seven men hold the floor, one after another,
and in the *Phaedrus*, though only two men are present, they deliver
three successive speeches which fill more than half the dialogue.
Usually, when reading Plato, we are listening in on an exchange
of questions and answers and are constantly thinking of better,
or at least different, replies we would have made. But in these
two dialogues we are treated like members of an audience from
whom nothing is required but passive attention. In each of them,
near the point where the preliminaries end and the speeches are
about to begin, Plato warns his readers that what follows should
not quite be trusted. The *Symposium* is presented as a report from
memory of a noteworthy occasion, but it comes filtered through
two different fallible recollections (178A), recounted by one man
who was not present at the original event but heard it from someone who was, and who repeatedly prefaces things said by the original speakers with the words "he said he said." Plato easily could
have written the dialogue as a first-hand report, or as a direct
dramatic presentation, but he chose to make it harder for us to
believe in the veracity of his writing. And early in the *Phaedrus*,
our attention is called to the fact that the whole following encounter between Socrates and Phaedrus takes place in the shadow of an
overarching plane tree (229A). The Greek word for that species of
tree is *platonos*, and if the first omicron is lengthened to an omega,
that word becomes the genitive of the name of Plato. If we picture
ourselves as present alongside the two speakers, *Platôn* is always
standing over us, the unseen author through whose imagination
the things we see and hear come to us. The topic of love, as Plato
treats it, carries with it a concern about speech-making, as well as
reflection on the effects of memory and imagination.

But in my experience of reading these dialogues, the warnings
don't stand a chance against the vividness of Plato's writing. The
excitement of a night spent as an audience to the leading lights of

the Athenian world of arts, learning, and politics draws us in, and so does the charm of a hot midday's idyll on soft grass, beside a cooling stream, under a shady tree. This drawing-in happens independently of any effect the topic of love may add to the mixture, and it is an instance of what Socrates in the *Phaedrus* calls *psychagôgia*, a power to move souls, which some people have by natural aptitude (260E–261A) and others by art (271C–D). This is the explicit concern of the second and shorter part of the *Phaedrus*: the question of what makes writing and speaking good or bad. A related question seems to lurk at the very end of the *Symposium* (223D), where, in the small hours before dawn, a sober and wide-awake Socrates presses a barely conscious Agathon and Aristophanes to admit that anyone who writes tragedies by art could write comedies, too. But this is a spot where the memory of the first-hand witness gives us very little to go on. Is Socrates suggesting to the two dramatic poets that their speeches about love were inadequate because each approached the task only from the point of view of his own specialty? That might be a hard claim to sustain, though, given the fact that the comedian Aristophanes offers a pessimistic account of love as a penalty for an original sin and fall of the human race, while the tragedian Agathon paints a rosy picture of love as all youth, beauty, and tender feelings. Socrates probably has something simpler in mind for the defining characteristics of comedy and tragedy. Aristophanes' speech, like all comedy, deals with humble matters in unpretentious words, and Agathon's speech seeks to elevate its subject by means of grandiose language. In various dialogues, Socrates uses the latter attribute as the sole reason for calling a definition, description, or piece of narration *tragikê* or *tragikôs* (as, for example at *Meno* 76E and *Republic* 413B and 545E), as if tragedy meant nothing but an exalted style of writing. So if we think of the comedian and tragedian as artisans defined by the tools of their trades, it may be that a combination of their skills would be needed to do justice to the topic of love. And might not the undeniable dramatic skill which is at work upon us in the dialogues be just what *is* needed?

It is certainly true that the speakers in the *Symposium* articulate a range of attitudes toward the heights and depths to which love may lead a human life, and in the *Phaedrus* Socrates steps from one side of this divide to the other to blame and praise love. Linking the two dialogues is the figure of Phaedrus himself. He inspires the speeches in the *Symposium* (177D) and provokes those in the dialogue named for him (242B). Though of the seven speeches in the *Symposium* his may seem superficial, by identifying love as the thing that most strongly reveals what is, in the first place, high or low, his speech starts a process by which a *logos* may be discerned and followed. A sexual attachment, he says, in both the lover and the one who is loved, in an older or a younger person, in a man or a woman, intensifies shame at behaving basely and a drive toward acting nobly (178D–E). In Phaedrus's speech, high and low mean noble and base, and we know what these are through the approval and condemnation we receive from others. Any worries about differences in opinion regarding what is considered admirable fade away when one is in love or is loved, because then the opinions of just one other person count the most. Phaedrus sees love as the guiding star that orients a human being toward the life worth aspiring to. Then the circle of approbation can widen outward from the love-partner to all those who are of the same sort, and who might be viewed as all right-thinking people. Now if this sounds naïve, that makes Phaedrus an appropriate choice to display the underlying, unreflective assumptions the people in the room bring to their thinking about love. In place of a definition of love, the *Symposium* begins with a look at it through the eyes of one person, and from that dramatic beginning a process of gradual re-examination can unfold. Phaedrus is the father of the discussion not only as the one who suggested the topic, but also as the one who brings it into being in a nascent state from which it can grow and develop.

The first response to Phaedrus's speech recollected and revealed to us is that of Pausanias, who begins by splitting the embryonic account of love in two. In so doing, he makes explicit the reliance on custom that was at work in Phaedrus's thinking. But as soon as customs are seen as variable and conflicting, custom itself can no longer serve as the ultimate guide to one's life; whatever it is that judges one custom as superior to another has tacitly taken over that guiding role. Pausanias turns on its head Phaedrus's fundamental attitude toward things. The issue that divides them is similar to one Socrates raises in the *Euthyphro* (10A); he asks whether the gods love holy things because they are holy or if those things become holy only because the gods love them. Phaedrus admires images in literature and legends of acts of courage and self-sacrifice inspired by love, and this admiration determines what he considers noble and base. Pausanias, on the other hand, looks down his nose at many who act under the influence of love, and he uses those feelings of disdain as the arbiter of nobility. People whom Pausanias considers inferior cannot do anything he would aspire to imitate. The idea that love is a universal and elevating experience appears as an absence of good taste. For Pausanias, the only love that can be worthy of praise is one by which people of refined taste reproduce their own kind. The ideal love is therefore the one between men and boys, in which men admit boys into a long-term intimacy that allows the older men to pass on their own ways of thinking (184C–185B). The virtue that Phaedrus associated most strongly with love was a courage that thrilled him with a vision of becoming better; the only virtue Pausanias speaks of is a wise, self-satisfied judgment by which he may make someone else better.

If one is looking for a pattern to emerge from the speeches in the *Symposium*, one might expect the next speaker to care most about either temperance or justice, since these, along with courage and wisdom, make up the traditional four cardinal virtues. As it turns out, the third speaker sees love as worthy of praise when it guides a life toward the good with temperance *and* justice (188D). But this speaker appeals to an unconventional view of those virtues, one that sees them as present in all animal digestion (187E) and in the weather (188B) as much as in human choice and action. In fact, the whole idea of high and low extremes as calling forth praise or blame is alien to our third speaker, Eryximachus. He is a physician whose art has taught him to see nothing as more desirable than keeping on an even keel. Phaedrus saw love as an upward impulse toward noble deeds, and Pausanias saw it as a desire to draw another up into his own image, but Eryximachus sees love as one among many areas of life in which bodily functions can become disruptive or be kept calm (186C). Eryximachus couches his speech in the language of cosmic principles, and it is difficult to see precisely how he intends those principles to be applied. A brief interlude that occurs before he begins to hold forth probably best illustrates his general idea (185D–E). Aristophanes, who was to have been the next speaker, is afflicted by a case of the hiccups, presumably because he had been too greedily pursuing his appetite for food and drink. Eryximachus offers him remedies to try, while he himself takes the next turn speaking. Only the remedy of last resort succeeds in relieving Aristophanes of his spasmodic respiration: he induces an expulsion of breath even more violent than his previous gulping inhalations by making himself sneeze. Intemperate ingestion had upset the even flow of respiration, which was restored by a complete interruption that allowed it to restart. The recommendation of temperate indulgence in food and drink is easy to infer and equally easy to apply to erotic appetites, but the love that Eryximachus ends up praising is not anything of which we have direct experience. Instead, it is the underlying, involuntary bodily processes that seek equilibrium and teach us to do the same. Love is best when it keeps itself unobtrusive. And how does this involve justice? Eryximachus understands justice as concord (187B) and communion (188D), the absence of conflict that can prevail when passions are quelled. Pausanias had praised love only after excluding its manifestations in most of the human race; Eryximachus takes that exclusion a step further. From his perspective, *any* human love can introduce a discordant note into the harmonious whole, though if it is justly tempered it need not.

Before yielding the floor back to Aristophanes, Eryximachus sternly warns him against making his audience laugh. Why he does this is unclear, especially since he does so in a jocular tone. Possibly he thinks the orderly thing would be a balance of seriousness in the speeches and levity in between them. In any case, Aristophanes has no intention of following Eryximachus's advice. He gives us a comic myth that is charming and funny but also contains a deep seriousness. The banter that precedes it does call attention to our laughter as worth thinking about in its own right. Aristotle says in his *Poetics* (1448b 36–38) that comedy attained its form when it stopped directing abusive ridicule only at particular persons and began to dramatize the laughable as such. Aristophanes' own comedies straddle the two sides of this transition. The demagogue Cleon is a frequent target of his mockery, and on one occasion (in the *Clouds*) Socrates is another, but most of Aristophanes' characters are fictional and represent ordinary Athenians, in one case (in the *Knights*), even under the name Demos, the ordinary crowd. The laughter called forth by these plays is primarily directed at the common frailties of human beings. Since the evening's speakers have all committed themselves to praising love, one must ask whether the same thing can be worthy of praise and deserving of laughter. The answer must somehow be yes, because most of those present are subjected at some point in the evening to good-natured teasing about their love interests or erotic prowess. In fact, the first words quoted by the dialogue's narrator appear to be a specimen of that same sort of raillery, directed at himself and based on nothing more than a similarity between the name of his district of Athens and the word for a certain body part. By admitting laughter into his praise of love, Aristophanes restores the human perspective that had been drastically narrowed by Pausanias and almost completely ignored by Eryximachus. That comic perspective opens the possibility that the truth about love may not flatter our vanity or display the virtues on which we pride ourselves most.

The dominant image in Aristophanes' speech depicts the robust exuberance of a being that can throw all four of its hands up in joy and turn cartwheels in any direction, facing forward and backward at once (189E–190A). This is not our condition, but it tells a story of what we once were and were always meant to be. That we have forgotten our true selves explains the pathos of our current condition, in which a pair of lovers can lie together, sated but still unsatisfied, heartsick at being unable to overcome their separateness and merge into one (192C–D). The myth explains our descent from our true estate as the result of an original act of rash and reckless ambition and pride. Our apparent wholeness included none of the virtues of character or intellect; in Aristophanes' account, the one thing needful was and always is piety (193A–B, D). Aristophanes joins in the general praise of love as the bringer of the greatest of blessings, but from his point of view its role as such is not because it lifts us to the highest good but because it provides an escape from the greatest evil. In his speech, Socrates will draw attention to the absence of the good from Aristophanes' vision, putting the words in the mouth of the wise woman Diotima (205E–206A). We are not what we were, and we sense that this means we can never fully be what we are, but the requited love that comes from finding our other halves is consolation. Contentment with our lot is piety, the piety our original roly-poly ancestors did not have. Acceptance of the world as the gods have given it to us is the best we can aspire to; after all, things could be a lot worse (190D). That is Aristophanes' comic vision.

Thanks to Aristophanes' earlier bout of hiccups, his praise of love ends up side-by-side with that of a tragic poet. But while Aristophanes' speech provides us with the laughter we expect from comedy, Agathon's does not arouse the feelings that tragedies normally evoke. What Agathon does give us, as Socrates remarks afterward (198C), is a rhetorical display in the high-flown style of Gorgias. Aristotle tells us in his *Rhetoric* (1404a 20 and following) that this was an old-fashioned way of composing tragedies, aimed at making simple-minded content seem impressive. It is particularly in the last third of his speech (197C–E) that Agathon lets the pure sound-effects rip, and they build an excitement in the audience that is released in thunderous applause. But, much as Aristophanes had done, Agathon begins by establishing a visual image, one that he borrows from Homer, of a divine being skipping across the heads of humans (195C–D). It happens that Homer is speaking not of *Erôs* the god of Love but of *Atê* the goddess of Folly, and that Agathon is not saying that Love flits across heads but that he steals into souls. The image does not fit the content, and Agathon tosses it out to the audience only to draw it back, leaving a general impression that associates tenderness with love, and garnishes his presentation with a few references to flowers. Between the visual and auditory sections of the speech, Agathon races through a set of mock arguments to the effect that the god of Love possesses all virtue. Agathon claims that Love is everything beautiful and good with imprecise images, specious reasoning, and a motley collection of balanced and assonant phrases. Agathon's performance is glib and assured, and as he himself says at its end (197E), his purpose has been to captivate his audience in a spirit of playfulness, a goal that he clearly achieves.

Only in the sixth speech does anyone makes a serious attempt to say what love is, and for this purpose Agathon's speech proves to be a useful prelude—by getting things exactly backward. Between their two speeches, Socrates quickly shows Agathon that the beautiful and the good are the things love longs for, strives for, and therefore must lack (201C). Agathon has confused love with the lovable and confesses to Socrates that he did not know what he was talking about. This knowledge of ignorance is a precious thing, which Socrates praises in Plato's *Meno* (84A–D) as the beginning of genuine learning, but here in the *Symposium* the pursuit of it is incompatible with the plan for the evening, with its demand for speechmaking.

Since he cannot go on questioning someone, Socrates casts himself in the role of the perplexed learner and invents a teacher to question *him*. Like the Eleatic Stranger in the *Sophist* and *Statesman* and the Athenian Stranger in the *Laws*, she is a foreign visitor, a Mantinean Stranger, and, like Timaeus in the dialogue of that name, she is an "honored one," honored in her case even by

Zeus, since that is the meaning of her name, Diotima. She completes the definition of love which Socrates had begun uncovering in his brief conversation with Agathon. Love is a desire for good things to be present now and into the future (200D), but Diotima adds one little word: *aei*, forever (206A). The primary contribution Socrates' fictional version of himself makes to his discussion with Diotima is to ratify the addition of *aei* by saying it is "as true as true can be" (*alêthestata*). But it is important to recognize that the "forever" she is speaking of is not the "happily ever after" of fairy-tale love; that would be a return to the untroubled peace and calm that Agathon envisages in the verse couplet that sums up his misguided first account of love (197C). Diotima's "forever" picks up the fierce longing not to be parted that Aristophanes had ascribed to all human lovers (192C), and she extends this thought to connect it with the strange compulsions irrational animals display in mating season (207A–B). She identifies love with the restlessness of mortal nature as such, in its drive to transcend mortality (207D).

Partway through the speech, the relationship between Socrates and Diotima shifts. He no longer presents himself as her partner in a dialectical quest. At 207C, Socrates says "you tell me" all about love, and from there to 212B, Diotima lectures to him, to the assembled audience, and to us, as someone supremely wise who is imparting her wisdom. Here the brightest of warning lights should be going off, since the first words Socrates had spoken upon his arrival at Agathon's house mocked the idea that wisdom could ever flow from the fuller to the emptier vessel (175D–E). To make sure we realize that a corner has been turned and a dubious new road is being taken, Socrates says that Diotima begins to speak like a complete sophist (208C); she even, briefly, breaks into verse the way Agathon had. But it is this stretch of the dialogue that all readers of the *Symposium* remember best, because it culminates in the most extravagant claim made in the dialogue, embodied in the image of love as a ladder by which human beings can ascend toward immortality.

One way in which a speech may justify its claims is to show that it sheds light on previous assertions about the same topic, and one point on which the five preceding speeches, with all their divergence, were agreed, was that love is a god. This was, in fact, the premise of the evening's speechmaking. Diotima begins (202E–203A) by modifying that idea but adopting its terms, locating love in a middle realm between the human and the divine. But in her lecture, she replaces that very distinction with the more precise notion of becoming and being. This is a philosophic topic that turns up in various Platonic dialogues (such as the *Theaetetus* at 152D–E), and its appearance here is one of the strongest indications that Diotima is an idealized figure and not an actual priestess. Mortal nature, as Diotima presents it, is more than the finitude of an existence that ends in death; it is, throughout life, a state of becoming in which everything that is present as a possession or an attribute, is slipping away all the time (207D–208B). What is truly divine is not the everlasting and age-less life envisioned by poets, but a state of being in which some-thing simply is what it is (211A). The doctrine Diotima imparts to Socrates claims that erotic desire comprises all the means by which humans seek to reach out from becoming to being. Sexual desire can lead to the generation of offspring that reach beyond their parents' lives, but Diotima tells Socrates that if he looks around him he will see that there is a variety of ways in which human *erôs* appears (208C), and as she reviews those ways we see the five pre-vious speakers reassemble before us. We see a lust for an undying name that Phaedrus spoke of as dearer even than life (208C–E), a passion for the imposition of order that Eryximachus singled out as the animating principle behind all the skilled and learned arts (209A), and an ardor to form and educate the souls of others that Pausanias saw as the ultimate concern of all lawgiving and custom (209B–C). As these three men spoke about sexual desire, each revealed some longing of his own that may embody an even stronger erotic drive. And while no such craving is directly evident in the speeches of Aristophanes and Agathon, both of them devote the primary energies of their lives to the writing of plays presented in public competitions, and they may look upon those plays as the "more beautiful and more immortal children" that Diotima speaks of (209C–D).

Diotima had explained that the name of love in its common usage separates off one part from the whole (205B). We cannot see the forest for the trees until we realize that sexual desire is only one form of lust, one impulse that drives us to seek our happiness with passionate ardor. But the image she finally offers us is not the forest of the dull cliché I just used, but a ladder (211C). What is happiness and how can we approach it? Think about the ladder. This is an image of a different sort than those our two poets made. Agathon gave us an image as ornamentation for an entertaining speech, and Aristophanes gave us a more apt image that brought his words to life. But nothing about the rungs of a ladder conveys either prettiness or liveliness. It is true that Diotima's word (*epanabathmos*) could be, and sometimes is, translated as "staircase," and a stairway to happiness has a more poetic feel, but it is the effort of climbing that her words focus on, and a ladder better captures her notion. Though it is here that she broaches her loftiest subject matter, she does so with an unpretentious and even inert visual aid. It may, in fact, embody that union of tragic and comic sensibilities that Socrates hints at in the small hours before the dawn ends the dinner party. In any case, Diotima's ladder seems to be an image meant to invite thinking. It does nothing at all for a passive hearer or reader who makes no attempt to interpret it. In this way, her use of it may serve as a remedy for her sophist-like pronouncements and for the limitations of any speech-making on topics that properly call for philosophic inquiry. Diotima's ladder of love is a memorable and uncomplicated image that can be carried off and thought about later. Her words, almost inevitably, set in motion a process of thinking, but anyone who is unsatisfied with those words might be stuck at the meaning of the bottom rung and go back later to think about why she insists that none of the higher loves is possible unless one has first fallen in love with one beautiful body (210A). And what does "higher" mean in the ladder image? Here it is no longer defined by the nobility of self-sacrifice in which Phaedrus saw love's highest manifestation, but by the self-fulfillment attained in contemplation of things as they are, now and forever (211D–212A).

An image like the ladder of love has to be unfolded because within it meaning is enfolded and inexplicit. If it is to be effective, such an image must lure the hearer or reader into a conversation. With whom is one conversing? Most immediately, with oneself, but also with the maker of the image: with Diotima, in the present case, and thus with Socrates, who speaks for her, and finally with Plato, the author who stands behind them both and who has drawn us into this quest for understanding in the first place. And if the image is tantalizing in its promise of containing something worth understanding, and exasperating in its unwillingness to say simply and directly what that is, the dialogue and its speechmaking may be left behind to generate a philosophic activity in their place. Diotima's transformation from questioner to lecturer to image-maker would then be complete, as new questioners come into being. And if the drive behind their questioning is strong, it might even be called erotic. But all such effects of Diotima's speech must depend on the memorable character of her image, because there is no room for them to be pursued in the following portion of the dialogue. The orderly progression of speeches about love is knocked irretrievably off-course by the arrival at Agathon's house of a new guest.

It is a common observation that since the *Symposium* consists of six speeches in praise of love and one more in praise of Socrates, the obvious suggestion is that Socrates is the embodiment of love. We may well be ready to entertain that thought with Diotima's speech in mind, but this should not keep us from recognizing the equally obvious fact that the man who arrives late and drunk and takes over as the life of the party would have a strong claim of his own to be regarded as the model of an erotic man. By his own account, Alcibiades considered himself irresistible to other men

(217A), and Plutarch's life of him tells us that he was a notorious seducer of women, including the wife of a Spartan king (XXIII, 7). In a speech reported by Thucydides (VI, 16 of *The Peloponnesian War*), Alcibiades glories in the fact that he entered seven four-horse teams in the chariot races at the Olympic games of 416 BC, a few months after Agathon's celebration, and took the first, second, and fourth prizes, showing the world by this unprecedented victory that fifteen years of war had not robbed Athens of its dominance. But Thucydides tells us that Alcibiades' ambition went far beyond athletic supremacy. He wished to be the conqueror who would bring both Sicily and Carthage under Athenian imperial rule (VI, 15). The Sicilian expedition that was to prove disastrous to Athens was launched in the following year, when Alcibiades fired up virtually the whole Athenian population with what Thucydides explicitly calls an *erôs* for the invasion (VI, 23). When we witness Alcibades praising Socrates, he is a man just reaching the height of his powers, who displays all the typical erotic drives, the ones we do not see in Socrates, appetites to dominate others sexually, athletically, militarily, and politically.

If Alcibiades himself presents the typical erotic nature, his praise of Socrates must enhance the oddity and eccentricity of the *erôs* that becomes apparent in the latter. And it is this very eccentricity (*atopia*) that Alcibiades singles out as most characteristic of Socrates (221D). Whatever one chooses to praise in Socrates will not have the same look about it as it has in others. To some extent, Alicibiades follows the usual pattern of laudatory speeches, praising Socrates for the four standard cardinal virtues—the same ones that Agathon attributed to the god of love. Socrates is obviously outstanding in wisdom (219D), but it is a wisdom of someone who claims to have no knowledge of anything (216D). He is clearly temperate, but it is a temperance that seems to have no temptation to overcome (216D–220A). And surely someone who argues that honors should be awarded not to himself but to another must be acknowledged as just; but what if, in all justice, he was the one who deserved those honors (220D–E)? And what about a courage displayed on the battlefield but at its utmost in retreat rather than in fighting, a courage that seems to have no fear or aggression to strike a balance between (221A–B)? If we look closely at Socrates, we might be compelled to admit that we do not know what the virtues are, even though we recognize their presence and aspire to them. In an erotic nature like that of Alcibiades, a nature that craves the highest distinction, these virtues are among the objects that one lusts to possess and to be honored for (218D).

But it is in connection with erotic matters that Socrates departs most from the norm, according to Alcibiades. The typical relation of lover and beloved is actually inverted in him, as Alcibiades learns by sad experience and of which he warns his friends (217C, 222B). We hear at the beginning of the dialogue that Socrates had lovers (173B) who followed him around and adopted his eccentric way of life, and it is through two such devoted lovers, Aristodemus and Apollodorus, that the report of Agathon's dinner party is transmitted to us in such loving detail. Alcibiades tells us that Socrates is lying when he claims he's irresistibly drawn to beautiful young men (216D, 222B). We, however, might note that he recognizes the lies Socrates tells as belonging to that special category known as irony (216E, 218D). What *that* might mean will become clearer when we discuss the *Phaedrus*. But even if there is no malicious intent in Socrates' erotic deception, Alcibiades feels humiliated by it. And there is a name in Athenian law for the arrogance that treats others in that way: *hubris*. Having been rejected when he threw himself at Socrates, Alcibiades tries to turn the tables by claiming that he is putting Socrates on trial before a jury of his friends for the crime of arrogance (219 C). This proclamation is all in good fun, but there is at least one layer of dramatic irony that we should hear in it. Alcibiades makes reference in passing to the sacred statues called Herms that stand all around Athens (215A), and to the secret religious rites practiced by those initiated into the Eleusinian Mysteries (215C, 218B). In the year following the dinner party at which he made this speech, Alcibiades becomes a fugitive from Athenian justice, condemned to death on suspicion that he took part in vandalizing the former and mocking the latter. According to Thucydides (VI, 15), it was the arrogance of Alcibiades' life and character that made people believe the accusations. Alcibiades' speech evokes some laughter (222C), but he may be one of those figures to whom only the combined talents of a comedian and tragedian could do justice. He describes himself as caught in something of a love triangle (216A–C), powerfully attracted to Socrates, who shames him, while he is pursued by the Athenian crowd, who flatter him but will ultimately turn on him.

From his own point of view, Alcibiades is a man very unlucky in his choice of love objects. Socrates rejects him first, with an extreme wound to his vanity, and soon the Athenian populace adds its total condemnation of his life. But Socrates would not agree that Alcibiades is a victim of bad luck. Socrates combined his rejection of Alcibiades' sexual advances with an invitation to the younger man to rethink his way of life (219A–B). The first images of lovers that we see in the dialogue, those of Socrates' followers Aristodemus and Apollodorus, show some visible ways in which people can transform their lives under the influence of love. One looks comical and the other sounds loony to those around them, but they are two examples of people whom love dislodged from their comfortable conventional lives and who took charge of their own pursuit of happiness. This suggests a theme reflected in various ways throughout the *Symposium*. Pausanias and Eryximachus, in their different ways, are smug men who see themselves as both mastering love and invulnerable to its power; one because of his political wisdom and the other because of his scientific art. Aristophanes preaches acceptance of things as they are and obedience to the gods as the lesson taught by the painful experience of love. Agathon paints the god of love as the perfection of an Athenian gentleman, a being of a delicacy and fineness not unlike himself. For Diotima, in contrast to all the others, the great power of love is to force us to confront our neediness, a recognition that leaves no room for self-satisfaction and no one but oneself to blame for a refusal to change (204A). Falling in love may be a passive experience, but climbing a ladder is a choice that requires an effort.

The ladder in the *Symposium* offers a way to collect into one view most of the participants in the dialogue, particularly those who represent what came to be called the golden age of classical Athens. In their differing ways, each elevated himself above the general run of humankind. Diotima implies that this was possible only because each was driven by a passion as intense and insistent as erotic love—in fact even stronger than sexual desire, since in each case that other passion took over as the principal motivating force driving a life. And she tells us that each of these lovers was in some fashion and to some degree overcoming, neutralizing, or negating the deterioration inherent in mortal life. But the image of the ladder also shows us that each of them *stopped* climbing before reaching the highest rungs. Even Socrates, who presents himself always as a learner and a questioner, has not fulfilled the highest human potentiality, unless he has done so on those occasions when he seems to withdraw wholly from his surroundings and become absorbed in thought (174D, 220C). Apart from Socrates, the distinguished Athenians on view in the dialogue have all chosen not to pursue any goal that might enhance the satisfaction their natural talents and naturally arising passions have brought them. Alcibiades may have greater imperial ambitions, but Socrates would consider them mere attempts at further pandering to the Athenian crowd. Socrates leaves us with the thought that a writer of tragedies could also be a comic poet, but could he, or a prominent politician, not *also* be a philosopher?

FROM THIS POINT of view, the *Symposium* is a dialogue that points to the cooling or fading of love, to people who stop striving and seeking at some arbitrary point and lose the capacity to change. But one exception to this characterization is Phaedrus. There is nothing smug about him, but we know of no notable attainments of his which might tempt him to be smug. He follows medical advice but does not attain the knowledge on which it is based

(176D). He talks idly about political reforms, but shows no sign of pursuing them (178E–179A). He cites and believes in stories poets tell, but is not moved to craft any of his own (179B–180B). He is still open to possibilities, less formed in character than the others, and that may be one reason why Socrates would choose to spend a large part of another day talking to him. Normally, in the dialogues, when Socrates is speaking with someone, numerous others are listening. He tends to draw a crowd, in part because they may hope to see Socrates embarrass someone. In the *Apology* (33C), Socrates admits that it is "not unpleasant" to hear unmerited pretenses of wisdom be punctured. But the tone of the *Phaedrus*, which takes place away from the competitive realm of the city, is relaxed and friendly. The first words of this dialogue are "dear friend," and nothing in the rest of work suggests that Socrates is anything but sincere about that, or that he has any ulterior motive for allowing Phaedrus to lead him out of his usual habitat.

In some ways, the *Phaedrus* may seem to be a continuation of the *Symposium*, since it begins with three more speeches about love. But it is not part of a sequence in the way the *Apology*, *Crito*, and *Phaedo*, or the *Theaetetus*, *Sophist*, and *Statesman* are. One might equally well see the *Phaedrus* as paired with the *Gorgias*, on the topic of rhetoric, or with the *Republic*, as an exploration of the three-part human soul. There are always multiple connections among the dialogues of Plato, and any such connection opens up a line of inquiry that may bear fruit. What one cannot do is assume that something said in one dialogue can be plugged into another, or detached from the context in which it occurs. Certainly anyone would grant that the things said in the dialogues are not typically dogmatic pronouncements, but are rather dialectical positions. And Socrates offers an explanation of the primary sense in which *he* uses the word "dialectic" in the *Meno* (75C–D). A debater would make a statement and say, "Refute it if you can," but the dialectical approach is to treat the other person not as an opponent but as a friend, ask him what he thinks, and proceed from that starting point. In the dialogues, Socrates customarily starts a discussion from where the other person is. And where is Phaedrus? Conveniently, the first line of dialogue presents this as the opening question of the *Phaedrus*: "Dear friend, where are you headed and where are you coming from?" And we get a literal and superficial answer, but we also soon get a deeper and more interesting one: he is on his way *from* hearing a composed speech delivered, *to* memorizing and having that same speech by heart. Near the end of the dialogue (275D–E), Socrates and Phaedrus agree that, however impressive any written speech may seem, all it can do when confronted with a question is keep stupidly repeating the same words. In one important sense, then, Phaedrus is going nowhere.

Unlike his companions in the *Symposium*, however, Phaedrus is presented to us as a man in motion, and although it is a motion guided by love, it may be that he is making no more progress than they, perched on the rungs of their achievements, are making toward a more enriching life. Early in the *Phaedrus*, the erotic preoccupation driving him is given a name (228C): he is someone with a lovesick passion for hearing speeches. Socrates applies this description to himself, but that is part of an elaborate trope in which Socrates claims to be seeing himself and his friend reflected in each other. And it is undoubtedly an apt description of the Phaedrus we observe in two dialogues. In one of them he gives a speech in order to be able to listen to more than half a dozen in return, and in the other he reads a speech aloud and provokes Socrates into giving him back two others. Late at night or in the morning or at midday, in town and out, in a group or with a single companion, Phaedrus, as Plato chooses to present him, is always eager to hear speeches. Even when he has the briefest of background roles, as in the mere mention of him in 315C of the *Protagoras*, Phaedrus is listening to a speaker and asking him for more; and this seems to be his distinction and claim to fame among his generation of Athenians (242B). Now I have already noted, at the beginning of this introduction, that Socrates does *not* love speechmaking, but considers it a misguided use of the power of speech itself, even if it is sometimes unavoidable. In the

Symposium, he tries his best to depart from the plan that calls for him to make a speech; instead, he starts a dialectical discussion with Agathon, once when Phaedrus interrupts him (194D) and a second time when he fulfils his promise to hold the floor the way all the other guests have. When Socrates switches to the mode of speechmaking, he tells a story about his young self as a learner starting off exactly where Agathon is at that moment. If Socrates is a lover of *logoi*—speeches—he surely does not have a craving to hear long ones, but rather friendly brief exchanges with a partner in conversation.

How then are we to understand Socrates' laying claim to a lovesick passion for hearing speeches? I think anyone who has read several of Plato's dialogues would be comfortable in saying that it is a lie. Alcibiades has told us that any time Socrates claims to be in love with any young man, he is lying. Given that he must start where his conversational partner is, when that partner happens to be Alcibiades, Socrates could surely find no firmer ground of agreement than that of adopting the pose of being as much in love with Alcibiades as the latter is with himself. And Alcibiades adds that Socrates has a way of lying all his own, his characteristic brand of irony (218D). Nowadays, the word "irony" can mean almost anything, literally from the sublime to the ridiculous. The Greek word for irony, *eirôneia*, started life as an innocent name for false modesty, the extreme opposite of bragging. Aristotle discusses *eirôneia* at the end of Book IV, Chapter 7 of the *Nicomachean Ethics* and pronounces it a "gracious vice," especially as Socrates practiced it. Others, such as Callicles at *Gorgias* 489D–E and Thrasymachus at *Republic* 337A, considered it a cruel weapon, but they are assuming that if Socrates is praising another or deprecating himself insincerely, that it could only be for the same reason they would do such a thing—to convey scorn. Callicles' mock-friendly advice at *Gorgias* 485E–486D and Thrasymachus's savage mockery at *Republic* 343A differ in tone and style, but they are both examples of ironic speech used to wound. The Greek words for this species of irony were *kertomia* (cutting to the heart) or *sarkasmos* (tearing the flesh). Rarely, if ever, in the dialogues does Socrates stoop to sarcasm. When his irony in the early part of the *Phaedrus* reaches its peak at 234D, and telling him to cut it out doesn't work, Phaedrus finally hits on an effective response at 236C–E by entering into the spirit of the game and giving as good as he gets. Somehow, accepting Socrates' irony allows Phaedrus to journey with him, and by 242A Phaedrus is already insisting that hearing a speech is not good enough, but a discussion of it is needed.

But is all this ironic rigamarole necessary? In the *Parmenides*, the young Socrates is treated to a dialectical display by the elderly philosopher for whom that dialogue is named, and it is a straightforward matter of making hypotheses and tracing their consequences. Parmenides takes a dialectical partner along with him, but only so that he will have a chance to catch his breath between questions while someone chosen for his docility provides the obvious logical answers (137B). The ultimate conclusion of the exercise, at 166C of the *Parmenides*, is that "whether the one is or is not, the one and the others, in relation to themselves and to each other all in every way are and are not and appear and do not appear," to which his young and tractable partner replies, "that is as true as true can be." The conclusion would presumably be the same no matter whether the two are friends or not, or whether either one of them agrees with the hypothesis from which the exercise began. Parmenides grants that most people would consider this tedious prattle (*adoleschia*), if not complete gibberish, but he is quite serious in claiming that it is the only road to philosophy (135D). He makes a reference to the erotic passion for philosophy (137A), but beyond the fact that he confesses that all such passion has died out in him, it is unclear what he means. He may be suggesting that the whole erotic drive must be cleared out of the quest for truth before there can be a pure dialectic and a trustworthy result. If that is his meaning, then his dialectic is as far from a Socratic one as the sarcasm of Callicles and Thrasymachus is from Socratic irony.

In the *Symposium* it is Alcibiades who offers an explanation of Socrates' irony (216D–E). Socrates has an inside and an outside, and they do not match. The outside is characterized most of all by two things: erotic desire for young men and ignorance of everything that matters. And Alcibiades has discovered that both those things are not only false, but also the opposite of the truth. Socrates is uninterested in the sexual gratification any young man might offer, and incomparably more intelligent and thoughtful than any Athenian whom people consider wise. The first of his two semblances has the effect of getting the attention of young men, and the second might give them the confidence to join him in a quest to know something as opposed to waiting for him to tell it to them. In that sense, his ironic pose is rhetorical; it is not intended to uncover a truth but to prompt an activity. When Socrates makes the claim he discusses in the *Apology*, that all he knows is that he knows nothing, this is false modesty and strictly a lie; the dialogues are full of things he explicitly says he knows. But on another level he is telling the truth, in saying "I need philosophy as much as you do, and you are capable of philosophy as much as I am." Dialectic, as Socrates practices it, requires that he not take over the opinions of another person and treat them as hypotheses, but instead persuade that other to venture out with him beyond the things he has already thought, and this irony-laden insistence that the two of them have the same need and the same love provides the transition from his rhetoric to his dialectic.

But when Socrates meets up with Phaedrus there is another approach to rhetoric lurking in their presence. Lysias's speech in praise of the non-lover has already aroused Phaedrus's lovesick passion for hearing speeches. This is the same Phaedrus who, in the *Symposium*, complains that poets have neglected the praise of love, and who claims in his own speech that love brings out the best in all human beings. But it is not the meaning of Lysias's speech or the proposition it advances that has Phaedrus excited. That is why Socrates diagnoses the cause of the excitement as a passion for speeches themselves, divorced from what they say. It is the contrarian novelty of Lysias's theme and the nimble-witted skill of the speech's execution that have Phaedrus so enraptured. And it is surprising to realize that nowhere in the dialogue do Socrates and Phaedrus *discuss* the content of Lysias's speech. That is addressed only by Socrates alone, outside the boundaries of the dialectical journey he and Phaedrus take, in one speech delivered with his head covered and a second speech that follows close on its heels, to remove the taint of the first without delay. *If* the three speeches are read as a continuation of the *Symposium*, they would link up with that dialogue at 210A–B, where Diotima asserts without explanation that it is a mistake to think one can skip the first rung of the ladder of love. Lysias's speech claims that cluttering up sex with love can do nothing but harm. I attribute this claim to "Lysias's speech" rather than to Lysias himself because he may have regarded his composition as a rhetorical challenge in the same way members of a debating society might. This may be the sense in which Phaedrus heard Lysias called a speechwriter as a term of reproach (257C), a wordsmith or ghostwriter who can deliver upon request a defense of any arbitrary proposition, at any length, truth optional.

Socrates, unlike Phaedrus, is unimpressed with Lysias's speech even when all its rational content is ignored (235A, 264A–E); he judges it to be the sort of work that a beginner might do, blundering in no order through his subject, piling up random points as they occur to him. At the beginning of his own version of the speech (237C), Socrates articulates the *logos* within the *logos*—the meaning within the speech—as the proposition that one should always enter into friendship with a non-lover in preference to a lover. This is not the proposition the original speech itself claims to be defending, which is about granting sexual favors. Socrates is tacitly claiming to have listened to Lysias's speech more carefully than Lysias himself has. As the random assortment of conclusions piled up in that speech, it was indeed friendship that turned up over and over as the greatest benefit to be had, and the one against which all choices were measured (231C, 231E, 232B, 232D, 232E–233A, 233C–D, 234A). Whether intentionally or not, Lysias's speech seems to set up a pair of divergent paths with lovers in one direction, friends in the other, and no way to have both. When Socrates recasts Lysias's speech, he places friendship along both paths, and also introduces a new criterion by which the choice between these friends is to be measured: the avoidance of the greatest harm, which would be the prevention of the pursuit of philosophy (239B). Socrates' recasting of Lysias's speech is not just a matter of improving the presentation of it, or strengthening its argument; it uncovers and makes apparent presuppositions that were not explicit in the original version. And among those presuppositions are assumptions about what love is and about the structure of the human soul.

In order to make the argument of Lysias's speech, Socrates must take love to be an innate, unrestrained, irrational desire for pleasure that tyrannizes the soul (237D–238C). This assumption leads him to classify *erôs* as a form of *hubris*. The latter word had a wide variety of meanings, several of which turn up in the *Symposium*; the sense it has here, and in most of its occurrences in the *Phaedrus*, is the one used by Pausanias for the sexual promiscuity that accompanies the vulgar sort of love. The meaning that has survived into our time, of being too big for one's britches and liable to be slapped down by the gods, is only one way of crossing the boundaries of decency and restraint. Three others, grouped together by Socrates with his cloak pulled over his head in shame, are gluttony, drunkenness, and erotic love. And there is a deeper presupposition underlying this conception of love, the assumption of a two-part human soul. Socrates spells this out by repeatedly using words that are neither singular nor plural but dual as he describes the pair of ruling and guiding principles in each of us, one a desire for pleasure, the other an opinion that strives for what is best. This was and is a common way of thinking, the idea that each of us is an unstable linkage of heart and head, led one way or another as one or the other of these powers gains the upper hand.

The image of the centaur, human from the waist up but a wild horse below, is the first of the mythical composite figures Socrates mentions at 229D when he tells Phaedrus that the primary concern of his life is to learn what kind of being he himself is. If love is to be given its due, it seems that the image of the centaur will have to be replaced with something more complex but potentially unified, not irredeemably dual, but perhaps tripartite.

The dominant image in the *Phaedrus* is, of course, that of two mismatched horses and their charioteer. It has inspired visual art of all sorts down through the centuries, and it probably overshadows even the considerable charms of the earlier and later parts of the dialogue in any reader's memory. It transports Phaedrus into a state of wonder at the astonishing beauty of this speech's craftsmanship (257C). Diotima's powerful image of the ladder of love cannot compare with it for complexity and sensory—and at moments sensuous—richness. In some ways, the chariot image of Socrates' second speech incorporates elements of Diotima's ladder. In the former, wings take the place of feet as the means of ascent. In each of the two a hierarchy of human lives and pursuits is established, though in the chariot image this is the result not of an upward climb but of a downward fall (248C–E). And this emphasis on the downward direction brings with it a considerable difference in tone and attitude. For Diotima, the bottom of the ladder is the beginning and always the foundation of the ascent to a fulfilled human life. But for Socrates, when he is speaking to Phaedrus and trying to undo the damage done by the false assumptions and general wrongheadedness of Lysias's speech, the lowest condition of the soul is the one toward which all weightiness and heaviness tend, the place where sophists and demagogues and tyrants live and flourish (248E). And along with these perversions and distortions of wisdom, justice, and courage, all the forms of *hubris* that lead to self-indulgence in carnal pleasures add their weight to a soul that might seek to rise. The image of the chariot contributes beauty to the conception of the three-part soul, and allows the imagination to do the work of interpreting it, but it may purchase these advantages at some cost to the truth, as Socrates seems to warn us (246A).

The charioteer is limited in the ways he can govern the other parts of the soul, his horses. He can give them their heads or jerk back on the reins—bestow freedom or impose slavery on those acts that might allow virtue or vice to gain entry, as Socrates puts it (256B). We hear nothing in the *Phaedrus*, as we do in the *Republic* (441E and following), about a harmony within the soul, an education tailored to each of its parts, or a mutual agreement that the rational part will rule. We hear only a bitter complaint from the unruly horse (254D) about the violation of the agreement the other two had made. The possibility of such an agreement suggests that each part could contribute something to the well-being of them all, but as Socrates tells the story, the unruly horse is never tamed but only broken; the repeated violent infliction of pain eventually makes his fear stronger than his desire, and he gives up his struggle (254E). In Socrates' direct exposition of his myth, the body is the soul's tomb (250C), and the unruly horse is nothing but a hindrance to the soul. But when Socrates fills in the details about falling in love, the explicit doctrine seems to be undercut. In the scene that begins in 253E, the chariot is at a distance from the beautiful beloved, the charioteer is feeling the first pangs of yearning, and the modest horse is standing still in an attitude of reverence. It is only the uncontainable lust of the unruly horse that, by brute force, gets the three of them close enough to see the loved one's face. This moment would seem to fit perfectly with Socrates' claim that erotic love is a gift from the gods, a divine madness that confers its blessings only on those who surrender to it, but he never puts the pieces together in that way. He praises the lover's madness but condemns the act to which it leads.

There is a maddening mixture of praise and blame throughout this speech that somehow reflects the maddening mixture of pleasure and pain that Socrates himself attributes to erotic desire (251D–E). The madness of the love felt as a desire for sexual union is said to be the only source of human happiness (253C), but the sexual act itself is called lawless and, when it occurs between two men, unnatural (*paranomos* and *para phusin*, 254B and 251A). The word *paranomos* here cannot mean literally in violation of law or custom; it must mean that sexual desire recognizes no restraint, and the combination of *nomos* and *phusis*, nature and convention, between them exhaust all possible norms. Throughout Socrates' second speech, the words that are consistently and repeatedly used for sex are *aischros* (shameful, vile, disgraceful, morally offensive) and *kakos* (bad, evil), and the combination of the two signifies the extreme opposite of *kalos kai agathos*, the phrase used for a perfect Athenian gentleman. Sex is spoken of not in the language of reasoned judgment but of antipathy and distaste. It sounds as though the white horse, who is governed solely by shame and honor, is doing the talking. And if we think back to the speech Phaedrus gave in the *Symposium*, he also determined high and low, praise and blame, by what is honorable or dishonorable in the eyes of others. Here, at the end of his second speech, Socrates warns him against the inhibition (*aneleutheria*) that most people praise as virtue (256E). It may be that the whole image of two horses and a charioteer was constructed to show Phaedrus a reflection of the particular biases and contradictions within his soul. Soon after the speech is given, we learn that Phaedrus considers bodily pleasures in general, especially those that mingle pleasure and pain, as fit only for slaves (258E). And with the winged chariot, Socrates paints for him a picture of a soul that soars above all such concerns. It happens, though, that Socrates dwells less on the soaring than on the growth of the wings (251A–252B), and his description of that is at least mildly obscene. Scholars have found in the beginning of this passage echoes of the love poetry of Sappho (from her fragment 31, the lines beginning *phainetai moi*). When Socrates does speak directly about the loftiest of matters, the ascent of the human soul to the realm beyond the heavens, the image he makes of the soul that has attained its highest aspiration is a charioteer with his head poked through the celestial sphere (248A). One may be reminded of the possibility that Socrates has raised, that the same poet could write both tragedy and comedy.

There is perhaps a hint, just before Socrates gives his second speech, that he will be departing from some of his usual ways of speaking and judging. To me, at least, it is jarring to hear him say (243C) that people who think all lovers are quick to feel anger and jealousy must have been brought up among sailors. It is true that in his lifetime, the occupation of the sailor had become synonymous with the lowest class of Athenian citizens, those who owned nothing but the labor of their own bodies. Since the time of the Persian wars, the power and wealth of Athens had grown as a result of the expansion of its navy and the introduction of a new kind of battleship called a trireme. From that time, every ship employing fifty rowers had to be replaced by a number of new vessels, each requiring one hundred and seventy, and there was abundant work available, at a good wage, for manual labor. What is surprising is the snobbish tone in which Socrates refers to the poor. It is identical to that of Pausanias in the *Symposium*, who cannot believe anything good could come of the undiscriminating love one ordinary, unrefined person might feel for another. In that dialogue, Socrates reminds his fellow banqueters that on the previous night they too were part of the crowd (194C). This is the more characteristic Socratic attitude, not that the poor are free of vices but that he and his privileged friends are not exempt from them. Similarly, the censorious attitude toward the natural sexual behavior of ordinary human beings that pervades his second speech is uncharacteristic of Socrates. Typically, it is Socrates who simply goes wherever an argument leads, even to examples that a proud professed hedonist like Callicles is too embarrassed to talk about in public (*Gorgias*, 494C–E). Though he adopts an uncharacteristically prudish tone in the second speech of the *Phaedrus*, Socrates remains his mischievous self when he makes the growth of the wings sound salacious. Socrates' serene attitude toward carnal pleasures in general is known to us from the testimony of

Alcibiades in the *Symposium* (218C–220A): deprivation of food does not bother him unduly, abundance of wine does not make him drunk, and the offer of sexual gratification neither tempts nor repulses him.

If there was ever a speech that cried out for discussion, the third one in the *Phaedrus* is it. Had it been given in some public place in the city, some aspect of it would surely have puzzled some listener enough to raise a question or an objection. But Phaedrus makes not the smallest gesture in that direction. His thoughts go immediately to the possibility of getting Lysias to make a new speech in response (257C). When Socrates asks if he wants to broaden the conversation out from Lysias to try to understand what makes writing good or bad in general, Phaedrus is speaking from the heart when he asks: "What other purpose is there for living?" (258E). But, though Phaedrus tries his best, he finds the more general discussion too bare or abstract (*psilos*, 262C) and is relieved to get back to the concrete example of Lysias's speech. The stretch of the discussion of rhetoric to which Phaedrus is able to contribute most begins at 266D, where his familiarity with the books and teachers of the subject allows him to take a larger part in the conversation. There is some similarity here to what happens in the *Theaetetus*, where the mathematician Theodorus is a very reluctant participant in the conversation about knowledge. Like Phaedrus, he objects to bare words (*psiloi logoi*, 165A), by which he means to include all philosophic talk. Socrates is relentless and gets him involved, and Theodorus eventually erupts in a spontaneous outburst about those who promote the doctrine of Heracleitus (179E–180B). In the second half of the *Phaedrus*, as in his talk with Theodorus, Socrates manages to find the level at which his dialectical partner has something of his own to bring to the discussion. In the *Theaetetus*, this tactic proves highly successful, but the obstacle to be overcome is not the same in the two cases; Theodorus was something of a misologist, a victim of a malady described by Socrates in the *Phaedo* (89D–E) as the result of having once trusted philosophic reasoning but turned away from it in disappointment, in his case to the safe certainties of mathematics. Phaedrus is a genuine lover of *logoi*, but he is the same kind of lover as the modest horse, one who stands still at a reverent distance from the beloved, unable to trust himself to make the first mad move. When Socrates urges him to turn the statements they had formerly made up and down to restart their questioning about rhetoric and make it his own, Phaedrus says he has the desire but cannot find any words in himself (272C).

Ought we to conclude that Phaedrus has enjoyed a couple of new speeches and diverted himself with a leisurely chat in the heat of day, while he has continued to be headed nowhere? It is at least possible that after some time spent contributing his book-learning to a conversation about rhetoric, he may be more invested in what he has heard than he would otherwise have been. And we might see the beginnings of a possible trajectory in the way Socrates' two speeches have prodded him beyond Lysias's speech. As he read Lysias's speech he glowed with delight (234D); after hearing Socrates' first speech, he was eager for conversation (242B); at the end of Socrates' second speech, we hear that he is vacillating on the brink of philosophy. He himself reports that he is full of wonder (257B–C). Socrates, of course, is the one who told the world that there is no road into philosophy except through wonder (*Theaetetus* 155D). It may be that Socrates has brought Phaedrus to the gateway of that road by making him progressively less satisfied with his own understanding of things. The two things that have become more puzzling rather than less in the course of the dialogue are love and rhetoric. Each of these topics involves the things that move our souls, and understanding them is entangled with our deepest assumptions about ourselves, so that nothing short of philosophic questioning could bring greater clarity about them. The first half of the dialogue centers around Lysias's explicit arguments that love is dispensable and we are better off without it. The second half revolves around the implicit claim of Lysias, in agreement with all the teachers of rhetoric, that truth is dispensable and plays no part in the decisions that govern our lives (260A, 272D–273A).

According to Socrates, the great merit of the madness of love is an enthusiasm that spills over to anyone close enough to the lover to share a friendship (255B–E). Even though Socrates seeks to wean Phaedrus away from his love of hearing speeches, it is the mad intensity of that love that draws Socrates out of the city to be with him. Socrates says much throughout the dialogue about his own dominant erotic passion, giving it a variety of names, ironic and sincere, playful and serious, but we have no difficulty recognizing it as what is called philosophy. In a sincere and serious moment at the end of the dialogue (278D), Socrates suggests that there may be something too pretentious about any claim to wisdom, and back when he first met up with Phaedrus (230D) he told us the name he may have considered most appropriate: he is a lover of learning (*philomathês*). In the *Republic* (475C), he merges the two notions into one in defining the philosopher not by any relation to wisdom but as "that person who's readily willing to taste everything learnable and goes toward learning gladly and in an insatiable spirit." The striking thing about this formulation, in the present context, is how well it fits Phaedrus. The only way it fails to describe him is by implying that he goes toward learning directly, without a detour through some knower, or more advanced learner, who could make a speech on the subject at hand, whatever it might be. Early in his second speech (245E), Socrates told Phaedrus that the true nature and definition of soul is that which is moved by itself. In the cosmological realm this applies in one way, and in the biological realm in another, but in the human realm the pre-eminent self-motion of the soul is toward knowing and is called learning. Like Socrates, Phaedrus never outgrew his appetite for learning, but unlike Socrates he allows deference to the opinions of others to inhibit its operation.

In much the same way as his dinner companions at Agathon's house climbed a ladder but did not climb as high as they might have, Phaedrus is presented as a soul who has grown wings but not flapped them and does not trust himself to soar. Viewed in this way, the two dialogues leave us with images of stranded souls, either halfway up a ladder but looking no higher, or winged but earthbound. This is not the usual way of reading these dialogues, but it has been brought into view by a faithful following of Socrates' advice to turn all his statements up and down and examine them closely. And doing so points the way for a reader to a reply to the Egyptian king Thamus, who claims that the only thing written texts are good for is to produce an appearance of wisdom in those who are ignorant (275A–B). We have looked at two books and found that they do not necessarily say the same things over and over if we bring questions to them. Some books, it seems, can present themselves to their readers the way Socrates presents himself to those around him, with an outside and an inside that may require some work to uncover.

Our efforts may also suggest a way to think about Socrates' claim that in every written text, the parts ought to be composed so as to fit with one another and the whole (264C). The perennial question that was asked about the *Phaedrus* in ancient times, and still provokes controversies in the philosophic journals of our own day, is how the dialogue measures up against its own standard; what is the unity of the *Phaedrus*? Like the centaur, it appears to be a monstrosity, with a front half about love jammed up against a back half about rhetoric. The question has remained a live one, not because there are no good answers, but because there are many.

The proposed answers I have seen are all good, in the sense that each of them leads a reader back into the dialogue, to find more connections and notice more depths. But if one expects a definitive answer that lays the matter to rest, I can say only that I have not seen it. Consider the magnitude of the task. The interpreter must find the necessary sequence that starts with a lover of speeches who is newly enraptured with a speech disparaging love, concludes as a written text disparaging all written texts, and reaches its highest point (as I would propose) in the description of a soul that gazes at the beauty it longs to unite with but holds back at a distance too great to permit it to see the beautiful one's shining face. If I were to pursue this question, I would begin with the observation that the unity of the *Phaedrus* must somehow be found in Phaedrus, if for no other reason than that there is no one else there with Socrates; the moves and steps he makes and takes in the discussion must all be called forth in one way or another by their appropriateness to Phaedrus. But the primary thing Socrates tells us about Phaedrus is that he is vacillating (*epamphoterizein*, 257B). Another possible way to translate that verb would be "trying to have it both ways." Phaedrus is driven by his love of hearing speeches toward those who compose them for law courts and legislative assemblies, and also toward those who pursue philosophic questioning. Athens in his lifetime provided an abundance of both, but Socrates tells him that, if he wants to satisfy his love, he has to choose to devote his life to one or the other with a whole heart. The attempt to live that particular double life seems to be the deepest source of a frustration Socrates sees within Phaedrus's soul. Would it be too perverse to claim that the unity of the *Phaedrus* is the duality within Phaedrus? It is Phaedrus who shifts the dialogue to the topic of political speechwriting, in the very act of declaring his admiration for Socrates' speech in praise of love (257C). Socrates' role is to lead the discussion where Phaedrus is willing to follow and capable of joining in.

But if Socrates is using a day spent outside of Athens to lead Phaedrus away from a preoccupation with the conventional rhetoric of his city, we witness Socrates making use of a different sort of rhetoric to do so. Just as Socratic dialectic is not the bare logic of Parmenides and Socratic irony is not the aggressive sarcasm of Thrasymachus, Socratic rhetoric is not that of Lysias. Socrates sketches out what it is in 277B–C. This rhetoric cannot speak to all human beings at once, but depends on an acquaintance with the listener. In fact, all three of these Socratic modes of activity, his dialectic, his irony, and his rhetoric, seem to be possible only in company with a friend, or at least a potential friend. Unlike the *Symposium*, in which we are shown a gallery of outstanding human figures, linked for one evening by their affection for Agathon, the *Phaedrus* focuses our attention on one relatively undistinguished person in all his particularity. When we think about his peculiarities, though, his lack of confidence in his own thoughts and his own voice, his excessive deference to the opinions and approval of others, we may find a certain universality in his portrait. Rhetoric designed to be inviting or provocative to him might turn out to be useful to others as well, and a dialectical beginning that sets out from his assumptions might soon link up with a path along which others could be traveling.

The road not taken, or at least not pursued for any great distance by any of the stranded souls in these two dialogues, is the dialectical one. In the *Phaedrus*, though, Socrates tells us a little about what might be involved in following it. This passage ends with one of his strangest statements about his own erotic passion. Calling himself a lover of hearing speeches was ironic, meant to be encouraging to Phaedrus; by observation we know that Socrates has the philosophic *erôs* if anyone does, and he gives us the rightful name of that passion when he calls himself a *philomathês*, a lover of learning. But in a very serious moment at 266B, he claims to be a lover of collecting and dividing the things we speak or think about. This two-sided activity requires bringing together a scattered multiplicity into a single comprehensive view, and then taking apart the resultant idea at its natural joints, rather than hacking away at it at random (265D–E). From the first of the speeches made in the *Phaedrus*, there is, as Socrates points out, a focus on the second phase of this activity and a dogged pursuit of "a sort of left-handed love." One might expect this to lead to conclusions that would need to be corrected, or at least re-considered, to restore a rightful balance. And is it not plausible that one place to look for a source of that balance is the *Symposium*? Diotima, beginning at 205B, insists that the way we speak about love misleads us by masking its unity, and in one breathtaking single sentence that soars from 210A to 210E, she guides our thoughts up the ladder to give us a comprehensive view. If we read both dialogues, we are left with a unifying vision of love offered in the name of Diotima; a critical rebuttal to any such vision, stemming ultimately from Lysias; and a warning from Socrates that we will find no answers in books to any questions we may have been stirred to ask.

THESE TRANSLATIONS have been made from the Greek texts edited by John Burnet, which are available in book form in the Oxford Classical Texts series and online through the Perseus Project of Tufts University. The only substantial departures from those texts are in the proof of the immortality of the soul at 245C–246C of the *Phaedrus*, and are noted in the footnotes there. A number of commentaries have been consulted, principally R. G. Bury's *The Symposium of Plato* (Cambridge, 1932), William S. Cobb's *The Symposium and the Phaedrus: Plato's Erotic Dialogues* (SUNY, 1993), and Harvey Yunis's *Plato: Phaedrus* (Cambridge, 2011). Readers who are curious about the controversy over the unity of the *Phaedrus* can find one of the most recent contributions to it in *Oxford Studies in Ancient Philosophy*, Vol. 43 (2012), and the earliest extant contribution, by Hermias of Alexandria, in a forthcoming book from Brill Publishers, *Plato's Phaedrus: Eros, Philosophy, and the Mysteries*, edited by Andrzej Serafin. I owe a large debt of gratitude to Eric Salem for once again making time when none seemed available to read early drafts and give me the benefit of his knowledge and judgment.

SYMPOSIUM

APOLLODORUS In my view, I'm not unprepared for the question 172A
you're asking. It just so happens that recently, while I was on
my way into town from my home in Phalerum, an acquaintance of mine caught sight of me from a long way behind, and
called out to me, making a joke out of his summons.

"Hey, it's the Phalerian member," he said, "Apollodorus,
won't you hold up a minute?"[1] So I stood there and waited.
And he said, "Apollodorus, you're just the man I've been looking for, to ask you about Agathon's get-together, and what the   B
speeches were that Socrates and Alcibiades and the other dinner guests made on that occasion about love. Someone else,
who heard them from Phillip's son Phoenix, was telling them
to me, and he said you know them too. But he wasn't able to
say anything clear, so why don't you tell them to me? You're

---

1. Earlier interpretations tend to find the joke in addressing someone by
the name of his home district, in the formal mode that would be used for a
member of a jury or legislative assembly, but recently Burt Hopkins has argued
convincingly that the humor must involve a pun on that place-name itself,
Phalerum. Doubling the lambda would mean Apollodorus is being hailed
first by reference to the word "phallus," which is the same in Greek as in English. See Hopkins's article "The Unwritten Teachings in Plato's *Symposium*," in
Epoché Vol. 15, Issue 2 (Spring 2011), pp. 279–298. It is worth noting that there
is some sort of relation between the openings of the *Symposium* and the *Republic*. There Plato's brother Glaucon is with Socrates when he is summoned from
behind on his way down from Athens to one of its ports; here it is apparently
the same Glaucon doing the summoning of another frequent companion of
Socrates on his way up to Athens from another of its ports.

the most suitable person to report the discourses of your close friend. But tell me first," he said, "were you present at that get-together yourself or not?"

C

And I said, "It looks like the one who told you about it got nothing clear at all if you think that get-together you're asking about was so recent that I could have been there too."

"I did," he said.

"How could that be, Glaucon?" I said. "Don't you know that Agathon hasn't lived here for many years, and that it's not yet three years since I began spending time with Socrates and making it my business to know what he says and does every day? Before that I was running around in every direction and thinking what I was doing mattered, when I was more pathetic than anybody, no less than you are now, thinking you ought to be doing anything and everything other than engaging in philosophy."

173A

"Stop making fun of me and just tell me when that get-together happened," he said.

And I said, "When we were still children, at the time that Agathon won the prize for his first tragedy, the day after he and his cast celebrated with a sacrifice."

"Very long ago, then, it seems," he said. "But who told you the story? Socrates himself?"

B

"No, by Zeus!"[2] I said. "It was the same person who told Phoenix, a certain Aristodemus from Cudathenaeum, a little guy who was always barefooted. He was there at the get-together, since he was one of Socrates' lovers,[3] and I have the

---

2. It is emphatic throughout the introductory portions of the dialogue that what we will be hearing is filtered through layers of intermediaries. Often throughout the narration that begins at 174A, Apollodorus will say literally "he said he said."

3. Male homosexual affairs were common and even fashionable among the upper classes in Athens at the time, and in this dialogue they are extensively discussed, both directly and indirectly. Typically, the lover (*erastês*) was an adult man who probably had a wife, and the beloved (*erômenos*) a boy in or not

impression he was among the most devoted of them at the time. But before long I checked out some of what I heard from him with Socrates, and he assured me that it was just as he reported it."

"Then why don't you tell it to me now? The road into town is a perfect place to talk and listen as we go along."

So while we travelled, we made those speeches the topic of our conversation. And that's why, as I said at first, I'm not   C unprepared for the subject. And if I need to tell it to you fellows too, that's what I ought to do. For among other reasons, whenever any philosophic discussions come up, whether I'm speaking myself or just listening to other people, and apart from any benefit I might expect from them, I take an extraordinary delight in them. But whenever any other sorts of talk come up, especially those of you rich money-grubbers, it irritates me and makes me pity you and your friends, who think you're doing anything that matters when you're not doing any-   D thing at all. Most likely you fellows consider me a miserable wretch, and I'm afraid you're right about that. But I don't just think that about you guys; I know it very well.

COMPANION You're always the same, Apollodorus—always running down yourself and everybody else. In my view it's simple: you think everyone is miserable except Socrates, starting with yourself. I don't know exactly why you were given the nickname "loony," but that's just the way your talk always sounds, when you berate yourself and everybody except Socrates.

APOLLODORUS So it's obvious to you, my very dear friend, that   E I'm insane and unhinged when I think such thoughts about myself and you gentlemen?

---

far beyond his teens. In 416 BC, the year Agathon won the prize that is celebrated here, Socrates would have been in his 50s. Whatever form of intimacy his circle of admirers sought, it could not have followed the conventional pattern.

COMPANION It's not worth arguing about that now, Apollodorus. Just stick to what we asked you and tell us what those speeches were.

APOLLODORUS Well now, they were something along these lines—but I'd better try to tell you the story from the beginning the way he told it to me.

174A

Aristodemus said he bumped into Socrates and found that he had just bathed and put slippers on his feet—not things that man did very often. And he asked him where he was going that he had made himself so beautiful. And Socrates told him "to dinner at Agathon's, since I steered clear of him yesterday during his victory celebrations, fearing the crowd, but I agreed to be there today. So I beautified myself like this to go in beauty to someone beautiful. But what about you?" he said. "How do you feel about going to dinner uninvited? Are you willing?"

B

And he said, "I assure you that I'll do whatever you tell me to do."

"Come along then," he said, "and we'll spoil the proverb by changing it to 'Good men go on their own to a good man's feast.'⁴ Homer may very well not only have spoiled that proverb but made a mockery of it, because after he'd made Agamemnon a man outstandingly good at warfare and Menelaus a 'feeble spearman,'⁵ he makes Menelaus go uninvited to the sacrifices and feast Agamemnon is holding, the worse man to the meal provided by his better."

C

And when he heard him say that, Aristodemus said, "I'm afraid the odds are that my case is not like your version, Socrates, but like that of Homer, with a worthless fellow going uninvited to a meal provided by a talented man. See to it that

4. The proverb is "Good men go on their own to an inferior man's feast." The word for "good man" would also be heard as a pun on Agathon's name: "Good men go on their own to Agathon's feast."

5. *Iliad* XVII, 587.

you have some excuse for bringing me, since I won't admit to coming uninvited; I'll say I was invited by you."

D

And Socrates said, "With two going down a road together, we'll decide what we'll say.[6] So let's go."

After some such banter, he said they headed off. But then as they went along the road, Socrates became absorbed in some thought of his own and fell behind, and when Aristodemus would wait for him, he'd tell him to go on ahead. And when he got to Agathon's house and found the door open, he said he was landed in a ridiculous position, since one of the household servants immediately met him and took him where the others were reclining, and he found them just as they were about to eat. And as soon as Agathon saw him, he said, "Aristodemus! You've timed your entrance beautifully to join us for dinner. If you've come for any other purpose, postpone it for another occasion, since I was looking for you yesterday to invite you but never managed to see you. But how come you aren't bringing Socrates to us?" And I turned around, Aristodemus said, but couldn't see Socrates anywhere following me. So I told him that I in fact had been coming along with Socrates, at his invitation, to dinner here.

E

"Beautiful," Agathon said. "You did just the right thing. But where is he?"

175A

"He was coming in right behind me. I'm wondering myself where he could be."

"Can't you go look for Socrates, boy, and bring him in?" Agathon said to a servant. "And you, Aristodemus, go lie back on the couch next to Eryximachus," he added.

Then Aristodemus said a servant was helping him wash up so he could take his place on the couch when another of the servants came and announced, "This Socrates stepped aside and is standing on the neighbors' porch, and doesn't want to come in, even though I called to him."

6. Adapted from *Iliad* X, 224.

"That's bizarre," said Agathon. "Call him again and don't take no for an answer."

B   But Aristodemus said he told him, "Absolutely not; just leave him be. This is a habit of his. From time to time he turns away and stands wherever he happens to be. He'll be here shortly, I'm sure. Don't bother him; leave him be."

"If that's what you think best, that's what we'll have to do," said Agathon, "but you boys go ahead and feast the rest of us. Just serve up absolutely anything you like without waiting for anyone to give you orders—which I never do anyway—and for now think of me and the rest of these people as dinner guests

C   here at your invitation. Take good care of us to win our praises."

After that, he said they started eating dinner, though Socrates had not come in. Agathon often wanted to send someone to call Socrates in, but Aristodemus wouldn't let him. And he arrived after what was, by his standards, no very long delay, when they were at most halfway through dinner. And Agathon, who happened to be reclining alone on the couch at the end, said, "Over here, Socrates; recline next to me so that,

D   by touching you, I might get the benefit of the wisdom that came over you in the porch. It's a sure thing that you tracked it down and you've got it, since you wouldn't have given up before you found it."

And Socrates sat down and said, "It would be nice, Agathon, if wisdom were the sort of thing that could flow out of the fuller one among us and into the emptier when we touched each other, the way water flows through a piece of wool from the fuller cup to the emptier one. If that's the way it works

E   with wisdom too, then I'm greatly honored by reclining next to you. I expect to be filled up with an abundance of beautiful wisdom from you. My own is a trifling thing, as unreliable as if it were a dream, while yours is radiant and boundless, and, young as you are, it came shining forth so splendidly just recently and made itself visible with more than thirty thousand Greeks as witnesses."

"You're a cruel man, Socrates," said Agathon.

"A little later you and I will submit these claims about wisdom to a verdict, using Dionysus as our judge. But for now, concentrate first on dinner."

After that, he said, when Socrates had reclined on the couch and taken his meal along with the others, and they had made libations and sung a hymn to the god, and done the rest of the things that custom prescribes, they turned to the drinking. And he said Pausanias started it off with a remark to the following effect: "Well, gents, how can we go easy on the drinking? To tell you the truth, I'm very much the worse for wear from yesterday's binge and I need some relief. I imagine that's true of many of you as well, since you were there yesterday, so think of a way we can ease up on our drinking."

Then Aristophanes told him, "You've got that right, Pausanias; we need to take every precaution to go easy on the drinking. I'm one of those who got pickled yesterday."

And he said that when Eryximachus, son of Acumenus, heard them, he said, "Right you are, fellows. And I want to hear from one more of you, from Agathon, about how keen on drinking he is."

"Not keen at all, for my part," he said.

"Well, it seems to me it would be a lucky break for us," Eryximachus went on, "for me and for Aristodemus and Phaedrus here, if you who are the mightiest of the drinkers are backing off from it now. *We*'re always weaklings. I leave Socrates out of account, since he's up to the task either way, and whichever way we go will be all right with him. And since it seems to me that no one here is eager to drink a lot of wine, perhaps you wouldn't take it so hard if I told you the truth about getting drunk. For in my view, one thing has become abundantly clear to me from the study of medicine, and that is that drunkenness is harmful to human beings. As far as it's within my power, I would never be willing to do any heavy

176A

B

C

D

drinking myself, nor to recommend it to anyone else, especially while he's still hungover from a previous occasion."

Then he said Phaedrus of Myrrhinus piped up and said, "*I* certainly make a habit of following your advice, and especially on medical matters, and so will the rest of our company if they're thinking straight." When they heard this, they all agreed not to make the present gathering a drunken party, but just to drink as they pleased.

"Well then," said Eryximachus, "since we've made this resolution that each of us will drink only as much as he wants, with no pressure on anyone, I propose next that we let the flute-girl who just came in go away and play her flute for herself, or, if she likes, for the women in the inner chambers, while we entertain ourselves today with speeches; what sort of speeches, I'm ready to propose as well, if you'd like."

They all said they would like that, and urged him to make his proposal. So Eryximachus said, "My statement begins with the words of Euripides' Melanippe: 'Not mine is the tale,' for what I'm going to say comes from Phaedrus here. Phaedrus is always getting worked up and saying to me, 'Isn't it strange, Eryximachus, that there are hymns and songs of tribute composed by the poets to any and all of the other gods, and yet in honor of Love,[7] so ancient and so great a god, not a one among all the many poets there have ever been has composed a single song of praise?[8] And consider our edifying purveyors of wisdom if you please; they've written prose eulogies of Heracles and

---

7. In this translation, "love" always refers to some form of the word *erôs*, and is never used for any other word. Greek had several words for various kinds of affection, goodwill, and friendship that might be comprehended in the broadest sense of love, but the point of departure for all the following speeches, in all their variety, is the primary and central experience of erotic passion.

8. R. G. Bury's commentary (*The Symposium of Plato*, Cambridge, 1932) cites as counter-examples the choral odes to *Eros* in Sophocles' *Antigone* (at 781) and Euripides' *Hippolytus* (at 525), but these confirm Phaedrus's point; they are not hymns of praise but acknowledgments of an invincible and overwhelming power of destruction.

others—the best of them, Prodicus, certainly has—and there is little to be surprised at in that, but lately I've come across a book by one of these wise men in which one finds salt getting amazing praises for its usefulness, along with many other such things that you can find extolled there.[9] Such a great to-do has been made about things like that, when to this very day no one of humankind has yet dared to make a hymn worthy of that name to Love, and so great a god goes so neglected!' And Phaedrus seems to me to be entirely right about this. So I'd like to gratify him by contributing my own dish to a buffet of speeches, and the present time seems to me to be a fitting occasion for us here to pay homage to the god. And if that seems good to you fellows too, we might find suitable entertainment in speeches. For it seems to me that each of us in turn from left to right ought to make as beautiful a speech as he can in praise of Love, starting off first with Phaedrus, since he's reclining at the head of the row and is also the father of our discourse."

C

D

And Socrates said, "No one will vote against you, Eryximachus; certainly I couldn't refuse when I claim that I have no knowledge of anything but love matters, and neither could Agathon and Pausanias, and certainly not Aristophanes, who devotes all his time to Dionysus and Aphrodite, and nobody else I see here could either. And while it may not give an equal chance to those of us reclining down at the end, we'll still be content if those who go before us give appropriate and beautiful speeches. So now with the best of luck, let Phaedrus commence and deliver his praise of love." And all the rest chimed in and encouraged him to do as Socrates said. Now Aristodemus didn't have a complete recollection of everything that each of them said, and I don't remember everything he told me, but I'll tell you fellows what seemed to me most worthy of memorializing in the speech of each one.

E

178A

9. A book by the rhetorician Polycrates contained praises of salt and bumblebees, among other things.

Phaedrus's Speech

First, then, as I say, he said Phaedrus started his speech from roughly this point: that Love is a great god, wondrous among both human beings and gods in many other ways but not least in his genesis. "For a god, to be among the eldest," he said, "is a high honor, and a sure sign of this is that Love had no begetter attested by anyone in poetry or prose. Hesiod says Chaos came first,

> And then broad-breasted Earth, an unfailing
> Resting place for all forever, and Love.[10]

And Acusilaus agrees with Hesiod that this pair, Earth and Love, came to be after Chaos. And Parmenides says of Genesis that 'first of all the gods she contrived Love.' Thus it is agreed by various sources that Love is among the eldest of things. And being eldest, he is responsible for our greatest blessings. For I can think of no greater blessing one can have from his earliest youth than a respectable lover, or a lover than a beloved boy. For the thing that ought to guide human beings through all of life, if they are going to live beautiful lives, cannot be provided by family ties, honors, wealth, or anything else as beautifully as by love. What do I mean by this? I am speaking of a sense of shame for what is shameful and an ambition for honor, for without these it not possible for either a city or a private person to accomplish great and noble deeds. I assert that any man who is in love, if he is revealed as doing something shameful or as suffering shameful treatment from another and, because of his unmanliness, doing nothing to defend himself, would not suffer as much pain to be observed by his father or his friends or anyone else as by the boy he loves. And we see exactly the same thing with the beloved one, that he feels shame to a heightened degree

B

C

D

E

---

10. *Theogony*, 116 and following.

before his lovers when he is observed being involved in some-thing shameful. So if there were some scheme by which a city or an army could be composed of lovers and the young men they love, there could be no better way to govern a city than theirs, by refraining from all shameful acts and competing for honor among themselves; by fighting side-by-side, even   179A a few such men could be victorious, one might say, over all mankind. For a man in love would surely be less willing to have the boy he loves see him deserting his post or throw-ing down his weapons than all the rest of his comrades, and would sooner choose to die many deaths. And as for leaving his beloved boy in the lurch or not coming to his aid when he's in danger—why, no one at all is so base that Love him-self could fail to inspire him to a prowess equal to that of the   B bravest man ever born. What Love provides out of himself to lovers is simply what Homer is speaking of when he says a god 'breathes fury'[11] into some of the heroes.

"What's more, only lovers are willing to die for others, and not only men but even women will do this. To the Greeks, no further testimony on behalf of this statement is needed than that provided by the daughter of Pelias, Alcestis; she alone was willing to die for her husband, even though he had both a father and a mother. Because of her love, she excelled them   C so much in devotion that she made them look like strangers to their son, related to him in name only. And when she per-formed this act, it seemed such a beautiful thing not only to humans but even to the gods that, among the many people who have performed so many beautiful actions, it is only to an easily counted few that the gods have granted the signal honor of allowing the soul to come back up from the realm of Hades, they sent hers up in admiration of her deed. And   D thus the gods paid the highest honor to zeal and courage on behalf of love. But Orpheus the son of Oeagrus they sent back

11. *Iliad* X, 482 and XV, 262.

from Hades' realm unfulfilled, after showing him the shade of the woman for whom he came; they would not give him the woman herself because they considered him unmanly, a mere strummer of tunes who didn't have the courage to die for love the way Alcestis did, but concocted a plan to get into Hades' realm alive. And it was for that very reason that they inflicted a punishment upon him and made his death come

E   at the hands of women. By contrast, they honored Achilles, the son of Thetis, and sent him off to the Isles of the Blest, because, though he had learned from his mother that he would die if he killed Hector but would go home and meet his end as an old man if he did not do that, he still had the cour-

180A   age to choose to take the side of his lover Patroclus and not only die to gain vengeance for him but join in death the lover who had already died. The gods were surpassingly delighted by this, and honored him prodigiously, because he cherished his lover so highly. And Aeschylus is talking nonsense when he says that it was Achilles who was the lover of Patroclus; Achilles was the more beautiful, in comparison not only with Patroclus but with all the heroes, was still beardless, and moreover was much younger than Patroclus, as Homer says.[12] For while the gods really and truly pay the highest honor to the courage

B   that grows out of love, their wonder and admiration are even

---

12. The reference to Aeschylus is to the play *The Myrmidons*, of which we have some fragments. Both Phaedrus and Aeschylus project their own customs and attitudes onto Homer's characters. There is nothing erotic between Achilles and Patroclus in the *Iliad*, a point Socrates makes in Xenophon's *Symposium* (which describes a dinner party different from the one depicted here) at VIII, 31. Homer's Patroclus grows up inseparable (*homou*) from Achilles since he was a little boy (*tutthos*) and Achilles even younger (*Iliad* XXIII, 84–85 and XI, 786); Phaedrus exaggerates by calling him "much" younger. At Troy they sleep in the same hut but at opposite ends of it, each with his own female companion (IX, 663–668). Achilles says "I cherished (*tiein*) him beyond all my comrades, equally with my own life" (*ison emê kephalê* XVIII, 81–82). Despite Achilles' superiority in looks, wealth, high birth, and prowess at war, Homer emphasizes the equality in their relationship, rather than the asymmetry between lover and beloved that Phaedrus is preoccupied with.

higher, and their rewards greater, when the beloved adores the lover than when the lover adores his beloved boy. For the lover is divinely inspired, and is therefore more godlike than the boy he loves, and that is why they honored Achilles more highly than Alcestis by sending him off to the Isles of the Blest.

"And so I declare that Love is the eldest of the gods, the highest in honor, and the most sovereign over the attainment of virtue and happiness by human beings both in life and after death."

Pausanias's Speech

He said that Phaedrus made some such speech as that, and   C that after Phaedrus there were some others which he did not remember very well. He passed over those and related the speech of Pausanias, who said, "It seems to me, Phaedrus, that our governing principle has not been well formulated in simply charging us to deliver praise of love. If Love were one, it would be fine, but in fact he is not one, and since he is not one, it would have been more correct to state first which sort   D we are supposed to praise. So I will try to straighten this out, starting by pointing out what we ought to be praising, and then delivering praise in a manner worthy of the god. Now we all know that there is no Aphrodite without Love, so if she were one, Love would also be one. But since she is twofold, then Love also is necessarily twofold. How could there not be two goddesses? Surely there is an elder goddess, a motherless daughter of Heaven whom we call by the name of the Heavenly Aphrodite, but also a younger goddess, the daughter of Zeus and Dione, whom we call Indiscriminate[13] Aphro-   E dite. Necessarily then, the Love that works hand-in-hand with

---

13. The word is *pandemos*, meaning common to all the people. Athens had a temple of Aphrodite Pandemos, and her worship is thought to have been introduced by Theseus when he united the separate villages of Attica into one political body.

the one goddess should rightly be called Indiscriminate Love, and the other Heavenly Love. So while we ought to praise all gods, we also ought to try to say what each of these two has as his allotted role. For this is how it is with every action; in its own right, the act performed is neither noble nor base. Consider, for example, what we are doing now, either drinking or singing or engaging in conversation. None of these things is noble in itself; it only turns out to be of that sort in the doing, by the way that it is done. When it's done nobly and rightly it becomes noble, but when done in a way that's not right it becomes base. So too, being in love, and the god Love, are not always noble or worthy of being praised, but only the Love that drives us to love in a noble manner.

"Now the love that goes along with Indiscriminate Aphrodite is literally indiscriminate and operates at random. This is the way ordinary human beings love. First, such people love women no less than boys; secondly, they are lovers of bodies rather than souls; and in the next place, they love the least intelligent people they can find, because they look only toward consummating the act and don't care whether the way they do so is noble or not. Accordingly, they end up doing this in ways that are good or its opposite alike, just at random. For this comes from the goddess who is the younger of the two by far, and has a share in both the female and the male by her birth. But that which comes from the Heavenly goddess has, first of all, no share in the female but in the male alone—and this is the love of boys; and secondly, she is the elder, and has no taint of promiscuity.[14] That is why those who are inspired by this

181A

B

C

----

14. The word translated here as "promiscuity" is *hubris*, a wanton or gratuitous overstepping of any limits of decency. It is the same thing Agathon playfully accuses Socrates of in 175E for the cruelty of his teasing. In Athenian law, the word referred to rape and also to any violent assault that involved causing humiliation as well as doing injury; in this sense it was regarded as a serious and sometimes capital offense. As Pausanias uses the word here, it may mean little more than "immodesty." See the note to 215B.

Love turn toward the male, feeling affection for what is naturally stronger and has greater intelligence. And even within boy-loving itself, one might recognize those who are under the pure influence of this Heavenly Love, for they do not love boys   D until they are already beginning to possess some intelligence, and this is when they are approaching the growth of a beard. For I am convinced that those who begin loving them at that point are prepared to be with them throughout the whole of their lives and make a life in common with them. They will not deceive a boy, making a conquest of him in the foolishness of his youth only to laugh at him as they leave and run off to another. There ought to be a law against loving young   E boys, to avoid the great expenditure of effort on an uncertain object, for there is always uncertainty with boys about what their outcomes will be, and which ones will end up in bad or good condition in soul and body. Good men willingly impose this law upon themselves, but the same sort of thing ought to be forced on those indiscriminate lovers, just as we force them as far as we possibly can not to make love to our free-   182A born women. It is *these* people who have brought discredit on love, leading some to go so far as to say it is a shameful thing to gratify lovers. They say that with their eyes on *these* lovers, observing their indecency and dishonesty, since obviously no action performed in an orderly and customary manner could rightly bring reproach.

"In other cities, to be sure, the custom regarding love is easy to grasp, since the distinctions are simple, though here and in Sparta the custom is complex. For in Elis and among the Boe-   B otians, and wherever there is no sophistication in speaking, it has simply been prescribed that it is a beautiful thing to gratify lovers, and no one, whether young or old, would speak of it as shameful; I imagine this is to spare them having the trouble of trying to win over the youngsters with persuasive words, since they're not adept at speaking. But in Ionia and in many other places where the people are governed by barbarians, it is prescribed that it is a shameful thing. For to the barbarians, on account of their tyrannies, not only this practice but also philosophy and a devotion to sports are shameful. For I don't suppose it is advantageous to their rulers to have high aspirations cropping up in those they rule, or any strong friendships or alliances, all of which love, supremely among all other things, tends to foster. This is something our tyrants here learned the hard way, when Aristogeiton's love and Harmodius's friendship became so unwavering a bond that it put an end to the tyrants' regime.[15] So where it's regarded as shameful to gratify lovers, this is a result of vice in those who hold that opinion, a jealous desire for power in the rulers and unmanliness in their subjects. But where it's considered noble without exception, this is due to a laziness of soul in those who hold *that* opinion. Here, things are regulated much more beautifully than in those cases, and in a way that is, as I said, not so easy to grasp.

"Just think about the fact that loving openly is said to be nobler than loving in secret, especially when that love is for a boy who is of the highest birth and best character, even if he may be more unattractive in appearance than others. Think too about how amazingly supportive everyone is of a lover, not as if he were doing anything shameful, and if he achieves a conquest, it is thought to be a noble thing, while if he does not, *that* is what's shameful. In the attempt to make a conquest, our custom grants the lover license to do extraordinary things to garner praise; if anyone had the nerve to do those things in pursuit of any other object and out of a desire to accomplish anything except this, he would reap the worst reproaches. If someone who wanted to get money from anyone, or gain some

---

15. Thucydides (*The Peloponnesian War* VI, 59) says, "The beginning of the plot of Harmodius and Aristogeiton was a result of lovesickness (*hê erôtikê lupê*)." That plot eventually led to the overthrow of the Pisistratid family of tyrants of Athens about a hundred years before the dramatic date of the dialogue.

ruling office, or wished for any other position of authority, and did the sorts of things lovers do in pursuit of their beloved boys, pressing their entreaties with beggings and pleadings, swearing vows, spending whole nights on doorsteps, and being willing to endure such servile slavery as no slave would ever accept, he would be restrained from acting that way by both his friends and his enemies; the latter would blast him   B for obsequiousness unbefitting a free man while the former berated him out of shame at his actions. But a lover who does all these things gets indulgent approval and is given leave by custom to do them without reproach, as a way of attaining an object wholly beautiful and right. And the most astonishing thing of all is that, according to the pronouncement of the masses of ordinary people, the lover alone is given absolution by the gods when he violates the oaths he has sworn; they declare an oath sworn under the influence of Aphrodite null and void. So absolute is the license that both gods and   C human beings have granted to the lover, as our local custom dictates. And from this one might conclude that being in love and being friendly to lovers is regarded in this city as something wholly beautiful and right. Yet when boys are beloved, their fathers put them in the custody of tutors and do not let them talk with their lovers, with particular instructions to the tutor on this point, and if the boy's friends of his own age see any such thing going on, they mock him, while their elders do not stop them from tormenting him or reproach them for   D speaking out of turn. Anyone looking at these things might think, on the contrary, that such behavior is regarded here as something utterly shameful. But here's what I think is really the point: it's not a simple thing, and as was said at the beginning, in itself it is neither noble nor shameful, but noble when it is done nobly and shameful when done shamefully. And gratifying a low sort of man in a low sort of way is shameful behavior, but it is noble to gratify a respectable man in a noble way. Now that indiscriminate lover *is* a low sort of man,

E   who's in love with the body rather than the soul, and just as he's in love with an unstable thing, he himself is unstable. The very moment the bloom of youth goes off the body he's in love with, *he* 'goes flitting off,'[16] with his many speeches and promises exposed for the shameful things they are. But the lover who is of respectable character remains faithful throughout life, merged into one with what is stable. Our customs are well

184A   designed and beautifully suited to test these lovers and distinguish those who should be gratified from those who should be avoided. That is the reason they encourage pursuit by the lovers and avoidance by the beloved ones, setting up competitions and criteria to detect which of the two forms of love is present in the lover and in the beloved. And this explains why, first of all, our custom considers it a shameful thing to be conquered quickly, so that there may be that interval of time which is thought to put so many things to the test so beautifully, and why, secondly, it considers it shameful to be won

B   over by money or by political power, whether the boy is recoiling in fear from some harsh treatment and can't endure it, or he's had some benefit done him in the form of money or the attainment of political ends and can't show it the contempt it deserves. For none of these things seems to be stable or lasting, not to mention the fact that they're not the sorts of things that lead to a lofty friendship. One pathway is left by our customs if a beloved boy is going to gratify a lover in a noble manner. For just as in the case of lovers it was seen to be nothing obsequious or blameworthy to submit willingly to any sort of slav-

C   ery whatever to a beloved boy, it is similarly our custom that there is one other form of willing enslavement, and one alone, that incurs no blame, and this is for the sake of virtue.

"For among us, it is established by custom that if anyone is willing to do service to another person in the belief that he will be the better for it in wisdom of any sort or in any other

16. *Iliad* II, 71.

part of virtue, this voluntary subjection is neither shameful nor obsequious. So these two dictates of custom, the one about the love of boys and the one about philosophy and the rest of virtue, must be coupled, if it is to turn out to be a noble   D
thing for a boy to gratify his lover. For whenever the lover and boy are headed toward the same place, each holding fast to his own guiding custom, the man who does any sort of service for a boy who gratifies him can rightly do so and the boy who returns any sort of favor to a man who is making him wise and good can rightly return it. And when the man has the capacity to put in a contribution toward wise judgment and   E
the rest of virtue, and the boy is desirous of acquiring education and the rest of wisdom, so that these dictates of custom cross paths in the same place, then there and there alone and in no other place, the boy's gratification of his lover coincides with being a noble thing.[17] And in this case there is nothing shameful about being deceived, while in all other cases the boy incurs shame whether he's been deceived or not. For if anyone provides gratification to a lover on the assumption that   185A
he's wealthy and for the sake of wealth, but is deceived and gets no money out of it when the lover proves to be poor, there is nothing any the less shameful about that; such a boy seems to be revealing his own character as one that will stoop to any service whatever for the sake of money, and that is not a noble thing. But by the same argument, if anyone provides gratification to a lover on the assumption that he's a good man, and that he himself will be better through his friendship with that lover, but is deceived when that man is proved to be base and devoid of virtue, the deception is noble all the same; this boy   B
too seems to be revealing his intrinsic character as one that would be willing and eager to do anything for anyone for the

17. The verbs in this passage that are translated "be coupled," "put in a contribution," "cross paths," and "coincides" are all similar in Greek (*sun* + *ballein* twice, *sun* + *ienai*, *sun* + *piptein*) and have the root senses of being thrown together, moving toward a point of intersection, and falling together.

sake of virtue and of becoming a better person, and that is the noblest of all things. And thus it is in every way entirely noble to gratify a lover for the sake of virtue.

"This is the Love that goes along with the heavenly goddess and is heavenly himself, and he is of great worth both to a city and to private persons, since he demands of the lover

C   himself and of his beloved that they exert great effort for the sake of virtue. But all other lovers belong to the other goddess, the indiscriminate one. These thoughts on the subject of Love, Phaedrus," he said, "are what I am able to throw together on the spur of the moment."

Pau-SA-nias paused SAY-ing this—the sophists have got me speaking in this sort of balanced phrases[18]—and Aristophanes was supposed to speak, Aristodemus said, but he happened to be having an attack of the hiccups, either from being overfull or for some other reason, and he wasn't able to take

D   his turn speaking. But the doctor, Eryximachus, was reclining in the next place down from him, and he said to him, "Eryximachus, you're just the man who can either stop me from hiccupping or speak in my place until I can stop."

And Eryximachus replied, "In fact I'll do both those things. I'll speak in your turn, and when you've stopped you can speak in mine. And while I'm speaking, the hiccupping may stop on its own if you can manage to hold your breath for

E   a long time; failing that, gargle with water. And if it's a *very* persistent case, take something you can tickle your nose with and sneeze; if you do that once or twice, then even if it's a very persistent case it will stop."

18. The word translated "balanced phrases" is *isa* (literally "equals"), and refers to a technique Aristotle discusses in the *Rhetoric*, beginning at 1410a 25. One of his examples could be translated as "longest on mopes and shortest on hopes," and someone I heard speak in the 1960s called certain moral attitudes "absolute and obsolete." Successive words or phrases are made equal in syllable count and similar in sound, with rhymes or any sort of assonance. There will be a virtual avalanche of such balanced phrases in this dialogue at the end of Agathon's speech, in 197 D–E.

"Then you can't start speaking too soon on my account," said Aristophanes; "I'll get on with doing those things."

Eryximachus's Speech

Then Eryximachus said, "Well, it seems to be incumbent on me, since Pausanias, after starting out his speech so well, failed to bring it to a satisfactory completion, to try to provide his speech with the conclusion it needs. For insofar as he said that Love is twofold, his analysis seems to me to have been beautifully made. But Love is present not only in the souls of human beings attracted to beautiful humans but also in other things that are attracted to many other things: in the bodies of all animals and in the things that grow in the earth, and one might even say in everything there is.[19] And I have gained the perspective, it seems to me, from our art of medicine, to see how great and wondrous and all-encompassing a reach this god has over matters both human and divine. And I will take the start of my speech from medicine so that we may give this art the respect it is due. For the nature of bodies has this twofold Love within it. For health and sickness in a body are admittedly distinct and dissimilar, and that which is dissimilar yearns toward and loves things that are dissimilar. The love that is found in a healthy body is one thing, and that which is found in a sickly body is another. And it is, as Pausanias was just saying, a noble thing to gratify good human beings, but a shameful thing to gratify those who are dissolute, and so too in bodies themselves, it is beautiful and necessary to gratify the good and healthy drives in each sort of body, and this is the very thing to which the name of med-

186A

B

C

---

19. Empedocles taught that all things are ruled by the twin powers Love and Strife (*Philia* and *Neikos*). Eryximachus assimilates these to the twofold *Erôs* described by Pausanias, and in order to harmonize the two perspectives he must broaden the meaning of erotic attraction (*erôs pros*) or erotic drives (*ta erôtika*) to encompass every sort of natural tendency, influence, or impulse.

ical art is given, but to gratify their bad and diseased drives would be shameful, and anyone who is going to be an artful practitioner must thwart them. To put it in summary fashion, that is exactly what the medical art is: a knowledge of the body's erotic drives toward states of fullness and emptiness.

D   And the supremely skilled physician is the one who can distinguish between these noble and base loves and make them change, so that the one sort of love is replaced and the other acquired. In bodies in which a love that ought to arise spontaneously is not present, someone who knows how to implant it and remove the love that is present would be a good practitioner. He needs to be able to take the most antithetical things in the body and make them be friends and love one another. And the most antithetical things are the contraries: cold and

E   hot, bitter and sweet, dry and wet, and everything of that sort. It was by knowing how to implant love and unanimity among these that our founder Asclepius, as these poets here assert and I believe, invented our art. And so, as I say, the medical art is

187A   entirely governed by this god, and in exactly the same manner, so too are the arts of gymnastic training and agriculture. And it is obvious to everyone who puts his mind to it even a little bit that music too is governed by the same principles as those arts, and perhaps this is what Heracleitus means but does not state very well by those words in which he says the One, 'at variance with itself, is in agreement with itself . . . as in the harmony of a bow or a lyre.'[20] Now it is utterly preposterous to say that a harmony is at variance or is composed of

20. From Heracleitus's fragment 51 in the Diels-Kranz numbering, with the subject "the One" apparently assumed from fragment 50. Eryximachus leaves out the important word *palintonos* ("back-stretched" or "straining against itself"), which precisely describes the paradox itself, in which the words for "that which is at variance" (*diapheromenon*) and "being in agreement" (*sumpheresthai*) are equated to generate and display their mutual tension with maximum force.

things that are still at variance. But perhaps what he wanted to say is that it is composed of high and low tones that were pre-   B
viously at variance, when they are later brought into concord by the art of music. For surely no harmony could be composed of a high and a low tone that are still at variance, because harmony is consonance and consonance is a form of concord— and concord of things at variance, so long as they are still at variance is impossible. But what is at variance and not incapable of concord can be harmonized, just as rhythm is made out of fast and slow things that were previously at variance but   C
later came into agreement. And just as the medical art introduces the concord in the former case, the art of music introduces it here, implanting a mutual love and unanimity. That is what the art of music is: a knowledge of the erotic tendencies involved in harmony and rhythm. And in the structure of harmony and rhythm themselves, the erotic tendencies are not difficult to discern, and the twofold love has not yet come to sight. But whenever rhythm and harmony need to be applied to human beings, either to one who composes them (which   D
people call song-writing) or to one who makes a correct use of melodies and verses that have already been composed (which is called education[21]), this is a difficult matter that requires a good practitioner. And the same argument comes back again: with orderly human beings, and so that those who are not yet in that condition may become more orderly, love between them ought to be gratified and fostered, and this is the noble and Heavenly Love that goes with the Heavenly Muse; but the   E
Indiscriminate Love goes with Polyhymnia,[22] and care needs

---

21. The word is *paideia*, not training in the art of music itself or in any particular skill, but the bringing to bear of all the muse-inspired influences that refine and civilize the soul. See Plato's *Sophist* (229D) and *Republic* (376E).

22. Eryximachus replaces the twofold Aphrodite of Pausanias's speech with a pair of muses, Urania and Polyhymnia (Goddess of many songs of praise), probably to contrast the one heaven with a multiplicity of any kind.

to be taken to administer him only to those to whom he properly applies, so that, when the pleasure he brings is enjoyed, no dissoluteness is introduced. Similarly in our art, it is a great task to make the right use of the cravings ministered to by the art of cooking tasty food, so that the pleasure may be enjoyed without sickness. So in the arts of music and medicine and in all matters human and divine, as far as humanly possible, we must be on the lookout for each of the two sorts of Love, for they are jointly present. Even the composition of the seasons of the year is filled with both these influences. Whenever the contraries I mentioned just now, the hot and the cold, the dry and the wet, attain an orderly Love toward one another, and take on a well-tempered harmony and blend, the seasons arrive bearing fruitfulness and health for human beings and the other animals and plants, and nothing can harm them; but when the Love that consorts with promiscuity gains the greater sway over the seasons of the year, he brings vast destruction and does them great harm. It is in such conditions that there tend to be plagues and many and various other diseases even among wild animals and vegetation; frost and hail and dry rot result from mutual overreaching and disorder in such erotic influences as the form of knowledge called astronomy studies in connection with the stars and their motions and the seasons of the year. Likewise, all sacrifices and rituals over which divination presides have to do with the communion of gods and human beings with each other, and these are concerned with nothing other than the safeguarding and healing of Love. For every sort of impiety tends to arise when someone gratifies or honors or venerates not the orderly Love but that other one in every action connected with parents, living or dead, or with gods. What is assigned to divination is the supervision and restoration to health of these Loves, and thus divination, as a knowledge of erotic tendencies in human beings and how they are condu-

188A

B

C

D

cive to decent observances and piety, is a craftsman of friendship between gods and humans.

"So manifold, so great, and, in sum, all-powerful is Love
in its wholeness, and when it reaches its completion in pursuit
of the good with temperance and justice, among both human
beings and gods, it is the supreme power and provides us with the
totality of happiness, enabling us to be in communion with one
another and even to be friends with the gods who are mightier
than we are. Now perhaps in praising Love I too have left many   E
things out of account, though that was certainly not my intent.
But if I have omitted anything, it is your job, Aristophanes, to fill
in the gaps. Or if you have in mind some other way of singing the
praises of the god, sing away, since you've stopped hicccupping."

Then, he said, Aristophanes took up the conversation, say-   189A
ing, "It has indeed stopped, though not before the sneezing
remedy was applied to it, which makes me wonder how the
orderly tendency of the body could yearn for such noises and
itches as a sneeze involves, since it stopped right away when I
applied the sneezing remedy to it."

And he said Eryximachus said, "Aristophanes, my good
man, look what you're doing. You're playing for laughs when
you're just starting to speak, and forcing me to monitor your   B
speech for anything laughable you might say, when you have
the opportunity to speak in peace."

And Aristophanes, with a laugh, said, "Right you are,
Eryximachus, and I take back what I said. And don't bother
to monitor me. What I'm afraid of about what's going to be
said is not that I might say something that gets laughs—since
that would be an advantage and on home territory with our
Muse—but something that makes you laugh *at* me."

"Aristophanes," he said, "you think you can toss out a
retraction and get away scot-free! Just keep your mind on what
you're doing and speak as though you'll be called to account.
Maybe, though, if I feel like it, I'll let you off."   C

Aristophanes' Speech

"Well, Eryximachus," said Aristophanes, "I do have in mind to speak in a different manner from that in which the pair of you—you and Pausanias—spoke. For it is my view that human beings have utterly failed to perceive the power of Love, since if they had recognized it they would have built him the grandest temples and altars and held the most magnificent sacrifices to him, but as it is, he gets none of these things, though of all observances, they are the ones that are most needed. For he is the greatest friend the human race has

D   among the gods, inasmuch as he is the protector and physician of human beings and heals those maladies whose cure would be the greatest happiness of humankind. I will make the attempt, then, to acquaint you with his power, and you will be teachers of it for others. You must first learn about human nature and its dispositions. For our ancient nature was not the same as it is now, but of another sort. For in the beginning there were three kinds of human beings, not the

E   two we have now, male and female, but also a third, additional one, having a share in both of those; its name remains to this day, though the thing itself has disappeared. For an androgynous being at that time was, in form as well as in name, a single thing having a share in both the male and the female, though it no longer exists except as a word applied as a term of reproach. Then too, the form of each human being was spherical all over, with the back and sides along a circle, and had four

190A   arms, the same number of legs as arms, and two faces, exactly alike, on a round neck. The two faces were situated on opposite sides of one head, and there were four ears and two sets of private parts. From these features, one might imagine all the rest. They walked upright just as we do now, but in whichever direction they pleased, and when they started running fast, they went head over heels with their legs out straight like tumblers turning cartwheels, and with the eight limbs they had

then to prop themselves up on, they went spinning along at high speed. The reason why there were three kinds of sexes   B
is that the male was originally descended from the sun, the female from the earth, and the mixture of the two from the moon, because the moon too shares in both natures, and they were spherical in themselves and their motion because they were like their parents. Now they were strong and hardy, formidably so, and got ideas above themselves, so much so that they tried their hands against the gods—in fact, what Homer says about Otus and Ephialtes[23] is also said about them, that they tried to make an ascent to the heavens with the intention   C
of attacking the gods.

"Then Zeus and the rest of the gods deliberated about what they should do with them, and they were at a loss. They weren't about to kill them off as they had done with the giants, striking them down with thunderbolts until they wiped them out, since that would mean wiping out their own honors and offerings that they got from the humans along with them, but they couldn't put up with their impious violence either. After long, hard thought, Zeus said, 'In my opinion, I've got a scheme whereby the human race could go on existing but stop its wild behavior by becoming weaker. I'll slice each one   D
of them in two right now,' he said, 'and so at one stroke they will become not only weaker but also more useful to us by the increase of their numbers. They will walk upright on one pair of legs, but if I think they are still behaving with impious violence and are unwilling to conduct themselves peaceably,' he said, 'I'll cut them in half again so that they go hopping along on one leg.' And with those words he began slicing the humans in two, the same way people slice sorb-apples for pre-   E
serves or hardboiled eggs with hairs. And on each one that he cut, he ordered Apollo to twist the face and half-neck toward

23. See *Odyssey*, XI, 305–320.

the incision, so that the human would be more orderly as a result of seeing its wound, and then he ordered him to heal up the rest. So he twisted the faces around, and pulled the skin together from all sides over what is now called the belly, as in a drawstring purse, and making one opening, what people now call the navel, he tied it off in the middle of the belly. And

191A

he smoothed away most of the other puckers and molded the chest with some such tool as shoemakers use for evening out the wrinkles in leather on the last, but he left a few on the belly itself around the navel to be a reminder of our ancient misfortune. Now that our nature had been divided in two, each human, yearning for its other half, would join with it, and they would throw their arms around each other and entwine themselves, longing to merge into one, to the point that they

B

began to die of starvation and of sheer inactivity, because they were unwilling to do anything at all apart from each other. And whenever any of these halves would die, the one that was left would seek out and intertwine itself with another leftover half, whether it met up with a half of a whole woman—that is, with what we now call a woman—or of a man; and so they kept dying off. Then Zeus took pity on them and put a new scheme into effect: he moved their private parts around to the front—for up until then they had them on the outside, and

C

they copulated and produced offspring not on one another but upon the earth, just like cicadas.[24] So he moved their privates to the front and made their procreation take place through them upon one another, by way of the male and within the female. And the purpose of these changes was that if, in their intertwinings, a man encountered a woman, they might generate offspring and propagate their kind, and even if a male encountered a male, there might at least be a satisfaction from

---

24. In the *Phaedrus* cicadas are involved in a different myth about an ancient race of human beings that died out (258E–259D). There the teller of the tale is Socrates, and the extinct portion of the human race was elevated to a divine role rather than falling from its original state.

their intercourse and they could finish it and turn back to their work and tend to the other concerns of their lives. This, then, is how far back the love of human beings for one another D goes and how deeply ingrained it is as a restorer of our original nature that strives to make one being out of two and heal human nature.

"Therefore, each of *us* is a broken piece, since it's filleted like a flounder, two out of one, each always seeking its own matching piece. All those men who are sections of the whole that was then called androgynous are lovers of women, and this class has given rise to many adulterers, as well as many E lascivious women and adulteresses. But those women who are sections of the woman have no interest in men at all, but instead are inclined toward women, and lesbians come from this class. All those who are sections of the male pursue males, and while they are boys, since they are slices of the male, they are fond of men and enjoy lying down with men and snug- 192A gling up to them; these are the best among boys and young men, since they are the most manly by nature. Some people say that they're shameless, but they are wrong; it's not out of shamelessness that they act that way but out of daring and courage and manliness, and an appreciation for what is like themselves. Here is a great proof: once they've grown up, it is only men of this sort who turn out to have an aptitude for politics. And when they are mature men, they are boy-lovers B and by their nature have no interest in getting married or producing children, but only do those things under the pressure of custom. They would be quite satisfied to live out their lives with one another, unmarried. In every way, then, such a man becomes a boy-lover and a friend of boy-lovers, a devotee all his life of his own kind. And whenever a boy-lover or anyone else meets up with that very one who is his or her own other half, they are wonderstruck and bowled over with feelings of warmth and closeness and erotic desire, and are unwilling, one C might say, to be parted from each other for even a little while.

These are the couples who remain with each other throughout life, though they could not even tell you themselves what
they hope to have from each other. No one would imagine
that this is just sexual intercourse, and that for this alone each
one finds joy in being with the other with such passionate
intensity. Instead, it is obvious that the soul of each is longing
for something else which it cannot put a name to, only dimly
divining and darkly hinting at what it wants. And if, when
they're lying in each other's arms, Hephaestus were to stand
over them with his blacksmith's tools and ask, 'What is it, you
humans, that you want to have from each other,' and when
they could not give him an answer, he asked them again, 'Is
this what you're longing for, to be united with one another as
much as possible, so that you are never separated from each
other by night or day? For if this is what you are yearning for,
I'm prepared to weld you together and forge you into the same
being, so that, from having been two, you become one, and
being one, live a shared life, both together for as long as you
live, and when you die, you will be one instead of two there in
Hades' realm, sharing a common death. Just see if this is what
your erotic desire is for and if it would satisfy you to attain
this.' We know that there is not even one person who, on hearing this, would reject the offer or claim to want anything else;
all would simply think they had heard what they were yearning for all along, to be united and welded with the beloved
in order to be made one out of two. The reason is this: that
was our original nature. We were whole, and the name for our
yearning for and pursuit of wholeness is Love. Before this, as
I've been saying, we were one, but now, because of our injustice, we have been split up and scattered by the god, the way
the Arcadians were by the Spartans. So there is reason to fear
that if we are disorderly toward the gods, we'll be split again
and have to go around like those figures carved in profile on
gravestones, sawed-off through our noses, turned into something like broken dice. So for this reason, we ought to exhort

all men to be pious toward the gods in all things, so that we   B
may escape the one fate and attain the other, with Love as
our leader and general. Let no one act in opposition to him;
and anyone who makes himself hateful to the gods is acting
in opposition to him. But by becoming friends of this god and
being reconciled with him, we will find and win the beloved
boys who are our very own, as few of those among us these
days do. And let Eryximachus not take me the wrong way and
turn my speech into comedy by saying I'm talking about Pausanias and Agathon. They may well happen to belong to that   C
class, and both of them are males by nature, but I mean this
to apply to everyone, both men and women: the way that
our kind can become blessedly happy is to bring love to ful-
fillment, each of us meeting up with his or her own beloved
and going back to our original nature. And if this is the best
thing of all, then necessarily the closest approximation to this
is the best thing available to us now, and that is to meet up
with a beloved who is by nature of one mind with oneself.
And if we want to sing the praises of the god responsible for   D
this, by rights we must give our praise to Love, who bestows
on us the greatest reward in the present by leading us to what
is our own, and also provides us with the greatest hopes here-
after, that if we provide the gods with our piety, he will estab-
lish us in our original nature, heal us, and make us happy
and blest.

"This, Eryximachus," he said, "is my speech about Love, of
a different sort from yours. As I begged you, don't start treating it like a comedy, but let us hear what all the rest have to   E
say, or rather both of the last two, since Agathon and Socrates
are left."

And he said Eryximachus replied, "I will take your advice,
since in fact I found your speech a pleasure to hear. And if I
didn't already know how formidable Socrates and Agathon are
in erotic matters, I'd be greatly afraid that they would be at a
loss for anything to say after so many speeches of every pos-

sible kind have been delivered. As it is, I still have confidence in them."

194A   Then Socrates said, "Your own entry in the competition was a beautiful one, Eryximachus, but if you were in the position I'm in now, or rather in the position I'll no doubt be in once Agathon has spoken too, you'd be well and truly afraid and in the same hopeless plight I find myself in now."

"You want to put a jinx on me, Socrates," said Agathon, "so I'll be thrown off my game by imagining the high expectation the audience has of my speaking well."

"I'd have a poor memory for sure, Agathon," said Socrates, "after seeing your brave and lofty bearing as you stepped onto the stage with your actors and looked straight out at such a vast audience, when you were about to put your own words on display and were not the least bit overawed by that, if I were now to suppose you could be thrown off stride on account of a few folks like us."

"What's that, Socrates?" said Agathon. "Surely you don't think I'm so full of theatricality that I don't know anyone with any sense is more frightened of a few intelligent people than of a crowd of fools."

C   "I'd certainly be doing you a disservice, Agathon," he said, "if I attributed any such unrefined opinion to you. I know very well that if you ever did bump into some people you regarded as wise you'd take them more seriously than the crowd. But we hardly qualify as that sort—we were present there too and we were part of the crowd. But if you bumped into others who *were* wise, you would in all probability be ashamed in their presence if you thought anything you were doing was shameful.[25] Is that what you mean?"

B

25. Note the ease and brevity with which Socrates has tacitly (and tactfully) denied the central notions of the speeches of Phaedrus and Pausanias. It is not the lover but the wise before whom he claims one feels shame, and he does not regard "present company," himself included, to be exempt from the common experience of the indiscriminate crowd.

"You put it exactly right," he said.

"But you would not be ashamed if you thought you were doing something shameful in the presence of the crowd?"

And then, he said, Phaedrus interrupted and said, "My   D dear Agathon, if you keep answering Socrates, it won't make any difference to him any longer what becomes of the task we've undertaken here, as long as he has someone to engage in a discussion with, and especially someone beautiful. And while it's a pleasure for me to listen to Socrates conduct a discussion, I'm under obligation to look after our praise of Love and to get a speech out of each one of you. So after each of the two of you has paid the god his due, that will be the time for your discussion."

"Your point is well taken, Phaedrus," said Agathon, "and   E there's nothing to prevent me from speaking, since there will be plenty of other opportunities for discussion with Socrates."

Agathon's Speech

"I want to begin by stating how my speech ought to be made, and then proceed to the speech itself. For all the previous speakers seem to me not to have made speeches in praise of the god, but rather to have made congratulatory speeches to human beings for the good things the god is responsible for giving them. About the attributes that belong to the god himself who has given these things, not one of them has spoken.   195A But the one correct method for all praise of every subject is to go through in speech the attributes of the one responsible for whatever sorts of things the speech happens to be about. Thus in the case of Love too, the right thing for us to do is to praise him first for what he is and then for his gifts.

"I assert, then, that while all gods are blissful, Love, if there is no impropriety or sacrilege in saying so, is the most blissful among them, since he is the most beautiful and the best. He is the most beautiful in the following respect: first

B   of all, Phaedrus, he is the *youngest* of the gods. He furnishes
a great proof of this statement himself by fleeing and hasten-
ing away from old age—obviously a swift thing itself, since
it overtakes us, at any rate, more swiftly than we want it to.
But Love by his very nature hates it and won't come within
miles of it. He's always in the company of the young and that's
what he *is*, since the old saying has it right, that like is always
drawn to like. So while I agree with Phaedrus on many other
points, I do not agree with this one, that Love is more ancient

C   than Cronos and Iapetus; instead I claim he is the youngest
of the gods and eternally young. That ancient history of the
gods that Hesiod and Parmenides tell happened under Necessity and not under Love, if they're telling the truth. Those
mutilations of one another, binding in shackles, and all those
other acts of violence would never have taken place if Love was
among them; there would have been friendship and peace as
there is now, ever since Love has reigned as king of the gods.
He is young, then, and not only young but tender. And a poet

D   such as Homer was would be needed to portray the tenderness
of the god. For Homer claims that Folly is a goddess and tender—at least her feet are tender—since he says

>   she comes on tender feet, and treads
>   not on the ground but on men's heads.[26]

In my view, that conveys a beautiful proof of her tenderness,
because she doesn't walk on a hard surface but on a soft one.

E   And we can make use of the same proof to show that Love is
tender. For he walks not on earth or even on our craniums,
which are not all that soft, but on the softest things there are,
and dwells in them. For he settles in and makes his home in
the temperaments and souls of gods and humans, and not in
just any and every soul; he steers clear of anyone who hap-

26. *Iliad* XIX, 92–93.

pens to have a hard temperament, and moves into one that is soft. So he is always in contact, not just with his feet but with his whole self, with the softest of the soft, and must necessarily be the tenderest of all. And in addition to being youngest and tenderest, he is supple in form. For he would not be able to enfold himself around a soul in every direction, or go unnoticed on his first entry into and exit from any soul, if he were inflexible. And the gracefulness which is universally acknowledged to belong to Love to an exceptional degree is a great proof of his well-proportioned and supple form, for ungracefulness and Love are always at war with each other. And the beauty of this god's complexion is indicated by his spending his time among flowering things, for Love does not alight on anything—a body, a soul, or anything else—that does not bloom or has lost its bloom. His place is among things that are in full flower and sweet in fragrance, and there he settles in and stays. 196A

"About the beauty of this god, even these remarks are sufficient, though many more are left out, but now one must speak about Love's virtue. The most important point is that Love does no wrong and suffers none, neither to or from a god nor to or from a human being. If he does suffer anything himself, it is not by violence, for violence has no effect on Love, and there is no violence in what he does, since everyone renders service to Love willingly. And anything done by mutual consent between willing parties is just, as 'the laws, the regal monarchs of a city,'[27] declare. And in addition to justice, he has the largest share of moderation. For it is agreed that moderation is a mastering of pleasures and desires, and also that no pleasure is stronger than Love. But if they are weaker, they would have

B

C

---

27. This overblown phrase is borrowed from the rhetorician Alcidamas. It may be found among the many examples of his writing that Aristotle gives in the *Rhetoric* (III, 3) to illustrate various aspects of badness of style, including "using adjectives not as seasoning but as the main course," and never using few words where more will do. Alcidamas was a disciple of Gorgias.

to be mastered by Love, so he must be their master, and by virtue of mastering pleasures and desires, Love must be outstandingly moderate. And as far as courage is concerned, against
Love, 'not even the god of war can hold out,' for Ares does
not hold Love in check, but Love—of Aphrodite, as the story
goes—holds Ares.[28] But the one who holds another in check is
the master of the one held in check, and the one who masters
the one who is most courageous in comparison to the rest must
be the most courageous of all. Now that the justice, moderation, and courage of the god have been discussed, the subject
of wisdom is left.[29] And one must try to the full extent of one's
powers not to leave that out. The first point, which permits
me to pay honor to our art as Eryximachus did to his, is that
this god is so wise a maker of poetry that he turns others into
poets. *Everyone* Love touches becomes a poet, 'even if he was
uninspired by the Muse before.'[30] And it is fitting for us to use
this fact as evidence that Love is a good maker in every form
of artistic endeavor in general that *is* inspired by the Muses.
For one cannot give another what one does not have, or teach
anyone else what one does not know. And who will deny that
the making of all living things, through which they are all
produced and born, is Love's special wisdom? And do we not
know that in the workmanship that goes into the crafts, an
artisan of whom this god becomes the mentor ends up well-re-
garded and a brilliant success, while one whom Love does

28. The quotation, which refers to Necessity rather than Love, is from a
lost play of Sophocles, *Thyestes*. The story in which Ares is caught in the act is
in the *Odyssey* (VIII, 266–369).

29. General opinion at the time gave preeminence to four or five virtues,
with piety sometimes added to the four mentioned here, and with *phronêsis*
used interchangeably with *sophia* for wisdom. In Plato's *Republic* (427E) and
Laws (965D), human excellence is treated as an organic whole made up of four
heterogeneous but interdependent parts, as opposed to a logical class that could
have as many members as fit under some definition. R. G. Bury cites evidence
in his commentary that Agathon is following an established rhetorical practice
in eulogizing someone by checking off these four boxes on a list.

30. A much quoted half-line from a lost play of Euripides, *Stheneboea*.

not touch remains obscure? Apollo surely invented the arts of archery and medicine and divination under the guidance of desire and love, so that even he must be a pupil of Love, and so must the Muses in music, Hephaestus in blacksmithing, Athena in weaving, and Zeus in 'steering the courses of gods and humans.'[31] It follows that the spheres of influence of the gods became established after Love took his place among them—love of beauty, obviously, since Love has no truck with what is ugly—though before then, as I said at the beginning, many frightful things went on among the gods, so we are told, under the reign of Necessity. But ever since this god came forth, all good things came to both gods and human beings from their love of what is beautiful.

    "Thus, in my view, Phaedrus, Love himself is the one who is first and supremely beautiful and good, and secondarily he is responsible for everything else of that kind in other beings. And I too feel an impulse coming over me to say a little something in metrical verse, for he is the bringer of

> Peace in the human world, calm in the seas,
> Winds in their beds, and troubles at ease.

He empties us of separation, fills us with participation, stirring us to draw together in all such gatherings with one another as this one; in feasts and dances and sacred ceremonies he becomes our leader—furnishing mildness and banishing wildness, lavish with charm but stinting of harm, propitious and auspicious, to the wise a glad sight, to the gods a delight, coveted by the loveless and cosseted by the love-blest, of sumptuous luxury, gracious and lavish, of pining and yearning the father and fount, devoted to good men, disdainful of bad, in stress and in fear, in pining and pleading, best steersman and

B

C

D

E

---

31. This is clearly a quotation, but the source is unknown. It contains a faint echo of a fragment of Parmenides.

shipmate and henchman and savior, glory of all, divine and human, peak of everything beauteous and good—all men ought to follow in his train, chanting aloud Love's beautiful strain, joining in the song he sings to captivate every single mind, both the human and the divine.

"So, Phaedrus, let this speech of mine be offered up to the god," he said, "the playful parts along with the fairly serious ones, blended to the best of my ability."

198A   After Agathon said this, as Aristodemus reported, there was thunderous applause from all those present for the young man who had spoken in a manner so becoming to himself and to the god. Then, according to Aristodemus, Socrates gave Eryximachus a look and said "Do you still think, child of Acumenus, that all this time I've been fearing a fear that posed no fear? Do you think it wasn't prophetic of me to say just now that Agathon would speak wondrously and leave me at a loss for words?"

"In my view you spoke true prophecy on one point, when you said Agathon would speak well, but as for your being at a loss for words, I don't believe that."

B   "My dear man," said Socrates, "how am I, how is anyone, *not* going to be at a loss at the prospect of speaking after so beautiful a speech has been delivered in such a medley of styles[32]? The other parts may not have been quite so wondrous, but who could not be struck by hearing the beauty of the words and phrases in the part at the end? When I reflected that I myself would not be able to say anything even nearly as

C   beautiful as they were, I was close to getting up and leaving out of shame, if I had anyplace to go. For the speech put me so much in mind of Gorgias that I was, without exaggeration,

---

32. Agathon's changes of pace make his speech fall neatly into three sections, 195A–196B, 196B–197B, and 197C–E, based on images, inferences, and assonances, respectively.

feeling what Homer describes[33]: I was terrified as Agathon was winding up that he would send the head of the dreaded Gorgias out to speak a speech over my speech that would turn me to stone and leave me dumbfounded. And I realized then how ridiculously foolhardy I'd been when I agreed with you all to take a turn among you at speaking in praise of Love, and   D
when I claimed to be an authority on erotic matters, because I knew nothing at all about the business of how one was supposed to make a speech in praise of anyone. For in my naiveté I imagined one was supposed to speak the truth about anybody one was praising, and with this as a starting point, pick out the most beautiful of those truths and present them as becomingly as possible. I was feeling quite proud of myself, thinking of how well I'd speak, assuming that I knew the truth about praising anyone. But it seems that this, after all, was not the way to give praise properly, which is instead to lay it on thick   E
in the greatest and most beautiful possible terms, whether or not that's the way things are; if it's a lie, that's no matter. It was taken for granted, as it seems, that each of us would pretend to be praising Love, not that he would be praised. And that's the reason, I suppose, that you fellows have been scraping all sorts of words together and applying them to Love, and declaring him to be this or that and responsible for so many other things, so that he might be made to appear the most   199A
beautiful and the best—to those who are ignorant, obviously, since it certainly wouldn't work for those with any knowledge—and your praise makes a beautiful and lofty impression. But I didn't understand the type of praise involved and it was in ignorance that I agreed with you to take my own turn at offering praise. The promise came from 'the tongue, not

33. In the *Odyssey* (XI, 633–635), Odysseus in Hades' realm, has a sudden realization that if he stays there he might see the head of the Gorgon, Medusa, which turned human beings who saw it literally to stone.

from the heart,'[34] so bid it goodbye. I'm not giving praise in
that manner—I couldn't if I tried. I am, however, willing to
speak the truth in my own way if you'd like, but not to stack it
up against your speeches, since I'd only be making a laughingstock out of myself. So, Phaedrus, see whether you want to listen to a speech of that kind, that speaks the truth about Love
in whatever sort of wording and arrangement of phrases may
come up as one goes along."

Aristodemus said that Phaedrus and the others then urged
him to speak in whatever manner he himself saw fit to speak.
"Well then, Phaedrus," he said, "indulge me a little further,
and allow me to ask Agathon some brief questions, so that I
can get some things agreed to by him and only then go on to
speak on that basis."

"I grant your request," said Phaedrus, "ask away." So after
that, he said, Socrates began at roughly the following place.

"My dear Agathon, in my view your lead-in to your speech
was quite beautifully done, when you said it was necessary
first to display what sort of attributes belong to Love himself,
and only afterward speak of his actions. I wholly admire that
starting-point. Come then, and tell me this about Love, since
you went through the rest of his attributes so beautifully and
impressively: is Love a love *of* something or of nothing? I'm
not asking if he is *of* some mother or father—whether Love is
an erotic desire for a mother or father would be a silly question—but just as I might ask about a father himself, is a father
a father *of* someone or not?[35] No doubt what you'd say to me,

---

34. Euripides, *Hippolytus*, line 612, where it is said of an oath.

35. Three uses of the genitive case are in play here. If "love of" means
"desire for" it is an objective genitive, but there is also the purely relational
sense in which "father of," like "taller than," must have some correlative term.
But Greek also used the genitive to denote parentage; what is translated "Eryximachus, son of Acumenus" is usually just "Eryximachus, of Acumenus" in
Greek. Socrates is deliberately making the question more confusing than he
needs to, and there may well be a brief silence here, with Agathon at a loss for
words before Socrates helps him get started on an answer.

if you wanted to give a beautiful answer, is that a father is a father of a son or a daughter; isn't that right?"

"Certainly," said Agathon. "And the same with the mother?"

He agreed to that as well.

"Answer just a few more questions, then," said Socrates, "and you'll have a better understanding of what I'm getting at. If I were to ask, 'and what about a brother—just as that very thing that he is, is he a brother *of* someone or not?'"

He said that he is.

"Of a brother or a sister?"

He agreed.

"Then try to tell me about love. Is Love a love of nothing or of something?"

"Of something, very much so."

"All right, then," said Socrates, "keep this thing carefully in your memory, whatever it is that he is a love *of,* and tell me just this much: that of which Love is a love, does he desire it or not?"

"Certainly," he said.

"And does he have that which he desires and loves and then desire and love it, or does he not have it?"

"It's a reasonable assumption that he doesn't have it," he said.

"Now put aside the reasonable assumption," Socrates said, "and consider whether it's necessarily the case for that which desires to desire something that it is lacking, and has no desire for it so long as it does not lack it. It seems amazingly true to me that this is a necessity, Agathon. How does it seem to you?"

"It seems that way to me too," he said.

"Beautifully said. Could anyone who was tall wish to be tall, or anyone who was strong wish to be strong?"

"That's impossible, based on what's been agreed to."

"And that's because he wouldn't be lacking in what he already was."

E

200A

B

"What you say is true."

"For if while being strong, he wished to be strong," said Socrates, "and while being swift, to be swift, and while being healthy, to be healthy—since someone might possibly imagine that people who *are* all these and such things and *have* all these and such attributes *do* desire the very things they already possess, and so I need to mention this to keep us from being misled—if you notice, Agathon, it's necessarily the case that these people have each of the things that they have in the present, whether they're wishing for them or not, and who could be feeling a desire for *that*? Instead, whenever someone says 'I'm healthy and I wish to be healthy,' or 'I'm rich and I wish to be rich,' and 'I desire those very things I already have,' we would tell him, 'you, fellow, have wealth and health and strength in your possession; what you wish for is to possess these things into the future as well, since at this present moment you have them whether you're wishing for them or not. Consider whether, when you say you desire the things that are present, you're saying anything other than that you wish for these things now present to remain present into the future as well.' Could he do anything but agree?"

He said that Agathon concurred.

"So then," said Socrates, "this is still a love of that which is not yet at hand for or possessed by him, a desire for it to be preserved for and present to him into the future?"

"Quite so," he said.

"And therefore that person, and anyone else who feels desire, desires something that is not at hand or not present, which he does not possess or is not himself or is lacking, and it is for such things that desire and love are felt?"

"Exactly," he said.

"Come then," said Socrates, "and let us recapitulate what has been said. And is that not, first, that Love is *of* things, which are, next, things of which a lack is present in him?"

"Yes," he said.

"Now with this in mind, recollect the things you said in your speech Love is *of.* Well, if you want me to, I can remind you. I believe you said something to the effect that things were established by the gods through a love of the beautiful, since there could be no love of the ugly. Didn't you say something along those lines?"

"I did say that," said Agathon.

"And that's a reasonable thing to say, my friend," said Socrates, "and if that's how it is, is it not the case that Love would be a love of the beautiful and not of the ugly?"

He concurred.

"And hasn't it been agreed that he loves what he's lacking   B
and does not possess?"

"Yes," he said.

"And therefore Love is lacking beauty and does not possess it."

"Necessarily so," he said.

"Well, then, do you call that which is lacking in beauty and possesses no beauty at all beautiful?"

"By no means."

"So if that's the way things are, do you still maintain that Love is beautiful?"

And Agathon said, "It's beginning to look as though I didn't know what I was talking about at all, Socrates."

"And yet you spoke so beautifully, Agathon," he said,   C
"but tell me a little bit more. Doesn't it seem to you that good things are also beautiful?"

"To me, yes."

"If, therefore, Love is lacking in beautiful things, and good things are beautiful, would he also be lacking in good things?"

"I would not be capable of refuting you, Socrates," he said, "so let it be the way you say."

"No, my amiable Agathon, it's the truth that you wouldn't be capable of refuting, since there's nothing difficult about refuting Socrates."

Socrates' Speech

D   "And now I'll leave you in peace, and turn to something I once heard said about Love by a Mantinean woman, Diotima,[36] who was wise about these matters and many others. There was a time, ten years before the plague, when she caused a postponement of the disease for the Athenians by having them hold sacrifices, and she was my teacher about things having to do with love. So I'll try to go through for you gentlemen the things she used to say, picking up from those things that were agreed to between Agathon and me, speaking myself by myself, making do as well as I can. So what I need to do, Aga-

E   thon, is first to go through myself, the same way you went through, what Love is and what sort of attributes he has, and then his actions. Now it seems to me that the easiest thing would be for me to go through it the same way the foreign woman went over it at the time she questioned me, since I was saying various things to her of pretty much the same sort that Agathon was saying just now to me, that Love must be a great god and must be among the beautiful things. And she pressed me with the same counterarguments I used with him, to the effect that by my own account he must be neither beautiful nor good.

"And I said, 'What do mean, Diotima? Is Love ugly and bad?'

"And she said, 'Don't let such blasphemy pass your lips! Do you think whatever's not beautiful is necessarily ugly?'

202A   "'Absolutely.'

---

36. To all appearances, Socrates invents this person on the spot. Her own name, combined with that of her city, suggests "a woman skilled at divination and honored by Zeus." Socrates has already bent the rules of the evening's entertainment by putting Agathon on the spot, after everyone present had been relaxed, listening to undemanding speeches. The fiction that Diotima becomes his questioner allows him to continue his preferred mode of discussion with no one but himself on the spot.

"'And anything that's not wise is ignorant? Haven't you noticed that there is something between wisdom and ignorance?'

"'What's that?'

"'Having the right opinion without being able to give a reasoned account of it,' she said. 'You know that's not the same as knowing—how could an irrational thing be knowledge? But it's not ignorance either, for how could something that coincides with the way things are be ignorance? And surely right opinion is just such a thing, between wisdom and ignorance.'

"'What you say is true,' I said.

"'Then don't force what is not beautiful to be ugly or what   B
is not good to be bad. And so too with Love; when you yourself concede that he is not good or beautiful, that doesn't make it any the more necessary for you to assume that he is ugly and bad,' she said, 'rather than something in between the two.'

"'But surely,' I said, 'everybody agrees that he's a great god.'

"'And by everybody,' she said, 'do you mean just those who do not have knowledge, or also those who do?'

"'Absolutely everybody.'

"And she laughed and said, 'How, Socrates, can it be agreed   C
that he's a great god by those who claim that he's not a god at all?'

"'And who might they be?' I said.

"'You, for one,' she said, 'I, for one.'

"And I said, 'How's that? How can you say that?' I said.

"'Easily,' she said. 'Tell me, don't you maintain that all gods are happy and beautiful? Would you dare to claim that any being who is not beautiful and happy is among the gods?'

"'Not I, by Zeus!' I said.

"'And by those who are happy, don't you mean those who are in possession of good and beautiful things?'

"'Certainly.'

D   "'But you've agreed that Love, from a lack of good and beautiful things, desires those very things, the things that he lacks.'

"'I have agreed to that.'

"'So how could he be a god if he has no share in beautiful and good things?'

"'Not in any way, it seems.'

"'Do you see, then,' she said, 'that you don't consider Love to be a god either?'

"'So what would Love be?' I said. 'A mortal?'

"'That least of all.'

"'What, then?'

"'As in the earlier examples, something between a mortal and an immortal.'

"'And what would that be, Diotima?'

"'A great inhabitant of the spirit world,[37] Socrates, for the whole spirit realm is between the divine and the mortal.'

E   "'Having what power?' I said.

"'That of interpreting and carrying messages to the gods from humans and to humans from the gods, prayers and sacrifices from the one side and from the other commands and benefits bestowed in return for sacrifices; being in the middle between the two, they fill in the gap and form the bonds by which the sum of things is held together, itself with itself. Through this medium all prophecy passes, and the art of

203A   priests involving sacrifices, rituals, and incantations, as well as

---

37. The phrase "inhabitant of the spirit world" translates *daimôn*. A common use of this word was for the guardian spirit that presided over the fortunes of a person or a family, making them happy (*eudaimôn*) or miserable (*kakodaimôn*). The English derivative "demon" picks up only the latter sense, but the former was the most common Greek word for "happy," and is used three times just above in 202C. In more than one of Plato's dialogues, Socrates speaks of a *daimôn* or *daimonion* that came to him as a voice when he was about to make a bad choice. Whether he meant that literally is, as always with Socrates, in question; a famous saying of Heracleitus (Diels-Kranz fragment 119) identified a man's *daimôn* with his character.

all divination and sorcery. A god has no direct contact with a human being; all interaction and conversation the gods have with humans is through this medium, whether we are awake or asleep. A man who is wise in such matters is in touch with the spirit world, while anyone who is wise in any other matter, any of the arts or handicrafts, is a mere mechanic. These spirits are many and of all different sorts, and one of them is Love.'

"'Of what father and mother is he born?' I said.

"'That will require a longer answer,' she said. 'All the same,   B
I'll give it to you. When Aphrodite was born, the gods held a celebration, and Resourcefulness, the son of Cunning, was there with the rest. And when they had finished dinner, as happens where people are having a good time, Poverty showed up begging, and she loitered near the doors. Now Resource-fulness had gotten drunk on nectar—for wine didn't yet exist—and he went into Zeus's garden and fell heavily asleep. Then Poverty saw her chance to deal with her own resource-lessness by conceiving a child of Resourcefulness, so she lay down by his side and became pregnant with Love. And that's   C
how Love came to be a follower and attendant of Aphrodite, since he was conceived during the celebration of her birth, and it's also the reason he is by nature a lover of everything con-nected with beauty, since Aphrodite is beautiful. And as the son of Resourcefulness and Poverty, Love has come into his station in life accordingly. In the first place, he is perpetually poor, and far from being tender or beautiful, as the common people assume, he is hard and dried up, barefoot and home-   D
less, always sleeping on the ground with no bedding or spend-ing the whole night in doorways or on the roads under the open air; having his mother's nature, he is constantly on inti-mate terms with indigence. But he takes after his father too, and he is a clever schemer for things that are beautiful and good, since he is brave and determined and quick to seize an opportunity, a crafty hunter who is always weaving some sort

E

of traps, a resourceful striver after wisdom who pursues philosophy all through his life, an expert with sorcery and drugs and sophistry.[38] By his nature he is neither immortal nor mortal, but sometimes in the course of the same day he blossoms and lives when he attains what he seeks, but dies at another moment, though he comes back to life by the power of his father's nature. But what he provides himself with is always slipping away, so that Love is never either devoid of resources or richly supplied with them, and he is in a middle ground between wisdom and ignorance. Here's the way it is: none of the gods engages in philosophy or desires to become wise—they already are—and if there is anyone else who is wise, he or she does not engage in philosophy either. But those who are ignorant do not engage in philosophy or desire to become wise either. This is exactly what is so problematic about ignorance; someone who has nothing beautiful and good[39] about him and is not wise is perfectly satisfied with himself. And so the person who doesn't think he's lacking feels no desire for that which he doesn't think he lacks.'

204A

"'Then who are the ones who engage in philosophy, Diotima,' I said, 'if they're neither the wise nor the ignorant?'

B

"'It's obvious by now, even to a child,' she said, 'that they are the ones between the two extremes, and Love would be among these as well. For wisdom is one of the most beautiful things, and Love is a love of what is beautiful; therefore Love is necessarily a philosopher, and since he is a philosopher he is in between wise and ignorant. And his origin is responsible

---

38. The last phrase contains words Gorgias uses to describe the power of rhetoric in his model oration *Encomium of Helen*, sections 10 and 14. In Plato's *Gorgias*, 465C, Socrates says that rhetoric and sophistry become indistinguishable in practice.

39. "Beautiful and good," *kalos kagathos*, was the self-congratulatory phrase the Athenian upper classes applied to their superior selves. Agathon used this combination of adjectives in the superlative in 197C to apply to Love, thus depicting him as the model of the perfect gentleman.

for these things too, since he comes from a father who is wise and resourceful and a mother who is unwise and resource-less. This, my dear Socrates, is the nature of this spirit. But the way you were imagining Love, it's not surprising you had the impression you did. You were assuming, as it seems to me, judging by the evidence of what you said, that Love was the beloved and not the lover, and I believe that was the reason it seemed to you that Love is wholly beautiful. What is lov-able is in actual fact beautiful and delicate and perfect and supremely blissful, but that which loves has an altogether dif-ferent look about it, of the sort that I have gone through in some detail.'

"And I said, 'Well you've certainly spoken beautifully, our visitor, but if Love is of that sort, what use is he to human beings?'

"'That is the next thing I'll try to teach you, Socrates,' she said. 'So, Love is of that sort and that is his origin, and he is, as you assert, a lover of beautiful things. Now suppose some-one were to ask us: "What is it that Love wants from beauti-ful things, Socrates and Diotima?" But it's clearer this way: the lover has a desire for beautiful things; what does he desire?'

"And I said, 'That they might become his.'

"'But your answer still yearns for further questioning,' she said, 'along these lines: what will the lover have if the beautiful things become his?'

"I said, 'I'm utterly unable to give any further answer off-hand to that line of questioning.'

"'But it's just the same,' she said, 'as if someone made the inquiry with a substitution, using the good instead of the beautiful, so try again, Socrates. The lover of good things has a desire; what does he desire?'

"'That they might become his,' I said. 'And what will the lover have if the good things become his?'

"'I have better resources to answer that question,' I said: 'he'll be happy.'

" 'Because it's by possession of good things that those who are happy *are* happy, and there's no further need to ask why someone who wishes to be happy wishes for that; the process of answering seems to have reached its end.'

" 'What you say is true,' I said. 'And do you think this wish and this love are common to all human beings, and that all people wish for good things to belong to them forever, or what would you say?'

" 'Exactly that,' I said, 'that they're common to all people.'

" 'Well, then, Socrates,' she said, 'why don't we say that all

B   people are in love, if all of them always love the same things? Instead we say some are in love and others aren't.'

" 'I wonder about that myself,' I said.

" 'Stop wondering, then,' she said. 'It's because we're separating off a certain form of love when we name it, and we attach the name love, that belongs to the whole, to it; and there are other cases in which we misapply other names.'

" 'Such as?' I said.

" 'Such as this one: you know that "poetry" is a multitude of things. For surely when anything whatever passes into being, from not having been before, the cause in every

C   instance is an act of making, so that the activities that fall under all the arts are acts of making and the craftsmen who perform them are all makers.'⁴⁰

" 'What you say is true,' I said.

" 'But all the same,' she said, 'you know that they are not called makers, but have various names, while one portion that is marked off from all making, the one having to do with melodic and metrical verse, is called by the name that belongs to the whole. For this alone is called making and only those who engage in this portion of making are called makers.'

---

40. The Greek word for poetry is *poiêsis*, which is also the general word for any kind of making. The English language once had in it the same ambiguity between specific and general senses of making, as is evident in the 15th or 16th-century Scottish poem *Lament for the Makaris*, by William Dunbar, in which the *makers* are all poets who died before Dunbar's time.

"'What you say is true,' I said.

"'Well, that's the way it is with love too. In its general   D
sense, any and every desire of good things and of being happy
is love—and its chief is Love almighty and all-entrapping.[41]
But those who take to it by various other routes, by way of
a craving for money or a passion for sports or a devotion to
philosophy, are not said to be in love or called lovers, while
those who ardently pursue it in one particular form get the
name of the whole in the words "love," "lovers," and "being
in love."'

"'It may well be that what you say is true,' I said.

"'And a certain story is told,' she said, 'claiming that those   E
who are in love are people who are seeking their other halves.
But my account asserts that love is not for a half or a whole
unless, my good friend, that happens to be something good,
since human beings are even willing to have their own legs
or arms amputated if those parts of theirs seem to them to be
doing them harm. I don't believe that people cherish things
just because they are their own, unless somebody is defining
the good as what is properly one's own and the bad as what   206A
is alien, since there is nothing else that people love other than
the good. Do there seem to you to be any others?'

"'No, by Zeus!' I said. 'Not to me.'

"'So then,' she said, 'is it true to say simply that human
beings love the good?'

"'Yes,' I said.

"'And what about this,' she said, 'must one not add that
they desire the good to be theirs?'

"'One must add that.'

"'And not only to be theirs,' she said, 'but to be theirs
forever?'

"'One must add that too.'

41. The beginning of the sentence is *to kephalaion*, which is picked up in
differing senses in the two clauses. In a logical sense, it is the broad and general
meaning of the word "love," and in a poetic sense it is the leadership of the god
Love. The source of the poetic phrase is unknown.

"'Summing up, then,' she said, 'love is for the good to be one's own forever.'

"'What you say is as true as true can be,' I said.

B   "'Now since this is what love is always for,' she said, 'in what manner do people pursue it and in what activity would zeal and effort be called love? What does this action happen to be? Can you say?'

"'I wouldn't be marveling at you for your wisdom, Diotima,' I said, 'and attending your lessons in order to learn those very things if I could do that.'

"'Well then, I will tell you,' she said, 'it is bearing offspring in the presence of a beautiful thing, by means of the body or the soul.'

"'One would need the power of divination to make out what you mean by that,' I said. 'I don't understand it.'

C   "'I'll say it more clearly, then,' she said, and she went on to say, 'All human beings are pregnant, Socrates, both in body and in soul, and when they reach a certain age, the nature within us brings an urgency to give birth. But it is impossible to bear offspring in the presence of something ugly, but only in the presence of something beautiful. Sexual intercourse between a man and a woman is a way of giving birth, and this is a divine matter; in this begetting and conceiving, that which is immortal is present within an animal that is mortal, and such things cannot come to be in anything out of harmony. But what is ugly is out of harmony with everything that is divine, while what is beautiful is in harmony. It is Kallonê who is present at childbirth in the guise of Moira and Eileithyia.[42] For these reasons, when anything that is pregnant comes into the presence of something beautiful, it becomes tender-hearted and melts into joyfulness and generates and

D

42. Moira and Eileithyia are goddesses who were called upon as protectors of women in childbirth, and whose title to that role is found in writings of Homer and Hesiod. Kallonê, from a variant form of the word for beauty, was, according to Seth Benardete, a name under which Artemis/Hecate was worshipped.

brings forth offspring; but when it comes into the presence of anything ugly, it shrivels up, becoming sad-faced and distressed, and turns away and coils up and does not generate, but represses its embryo and has a hard time with it. Hence for one who is pregnant and already heavily swollen, a great excitement is felt for what is beautiful, since the one who possesses it can bring release from intense pain. For, Socrates,' she said, 'love is not for the beautiful, as you think it is.' E

"'But what then?'

"'For generating and bearing offspring in the presence of the beautiful.'

"'Ah, well,' I said.

"'There's no doubt about it,' she said, 'and why for generating? Because generation is something eternal and immortal within what is mortal. It necessarily follows from the things 207A that have been agreed to that there is a desire for immortality along with the good, if love is for the good to be one's own forever. So the necessary result of our argument is that love is for immortality as well.'

"She taught me all these things, then, on the occasions when she would make her speeches on things related to love, and once she asked the question, 'What do you think is the cause of this love and desire, Socrates? Or haven't you noticed how strangely all the beasts are affected when they desire to produce offspring? Those that go on foot and the winged ones alike are all sick in the grip of erotic desire, first to mate B with each other and then to provide food for the newborn, on whose behalf even the weakest of them are ready to fight it out with the strongest opponents, even at the cost of their own lives; they are ready to endure the torments of hunger themselves in order to nourish those offspring, and there is nothing they won't do. In the case of human beings,' she said, 'one might imagine they do these things from rational motives, but for the beasts, what is it that causes them to be affected this way under the influence of love? Can you say?' C

"And I said again that I didn't know, and she replied, 'Do you expect that you can ever become an expert on matters of love if you don't put your mind to these questions?'

"'But that's exactly the reason I keep coming to you, Diotima, as I was just saying, because I realized I need teachers. So you tell me the cause of these things and everything else that has to do with love.'

"'Well,' she said, 'if you're persuaded that love is by nature a desire for that which we have repeatedly agreed it is, you can stop your wondering. For here again, by the same argument as in that case, the mortal nature is seeking to be, as far as is possible, everlasting and immortal. And for this nature, these things are possible only through the process of generation, by which it is always leaving behind another new being in place of the old one, even during the time when each one of the animals is alive and is spoken of as being the same. For instance, a human being is said to be the same person from childhood until reaching old age, though he is never in possession of the same attributes within himself, despite being called the same; he is continually becoming new while losing some attributes, with respect to his hair, his skin, his bones, his blood, and his whole body. And not just in his body but in his soul as well, his ways, his states of character, his opinions, desires, pleasures, pains, and fears never remain the same in each person, but some of them are always coming into being while others pass away. And what is much more unsettling even than this is that, with the kinds of knowledge as well, it is not only the case that some are coming to be in us while others pass away, so that we are never the same even in respect to the kinds of things we know, but every single item of knowledge is affected in the same way. For what is called *studying* shows that knowledge is slipping away, since forgetting is an outflow of knowledge and studying preserves that knowledge by a continual replacement of the departed memory with a fresh one that seems to be the same. And this is the way that every mortal thing is preserved, not by continuously being completely the same in the way something divine is, but by leaving behind, in place of what has aged and departed, something different and new that is just like it was. By this process, Socrates,' she said, 'a mortal thing partakes of immortality, both in its body and in all other respects, and it is incapable of doing so by any other means. So don't be surprised if every being naturally prizes its own offspring, since it is for the sake of immortality that this zeal and erotic passion are found in them all.'   B

"And when I heard this speech, I was left in wonder, and I spoke up and said, 'Aha, most wise Diotima, so that's the truth of the matter?'

"And she, just like the consummate purveyors of wisdom, said, 'Be certain of it, Socrates. And if you care to take a look at the ambition for honor among human beings, you'll be astonished at the irrationality of it if you don't keep in mind the things I've been saying, and take to heart how fiercely they are driven by an erotic passion to make a name for themselves "and store up undying fame for time everlasting,"[43] and how, for the sake of this, they are ready to dare all dangers, even more than they would on behalf of their children, and to spend money, slave away at labors of any and every kind, and even give up their lives. Do you imagine,' she said, 'that Alcestis would have died in place of Admetus, or Achilles would have died to avenge Patroclus, or your own Codrus[44] would have died to secure the kingdom for his children if they had not believed that an undying remembrance for virtue would be theirs, a remembrance we preserve to this very day? Far from it,' she said, 'but I do believe that all people do all things for the sake of immortal virtue and for such illustrious acclaim,   C   D

---

43. Commentators note that Diotima appears to break out in verse of her own making here, as Agathon had done in 197C, and her language is nearly metrical again in short stretches of sections D and E of 208.

44. An ancient king of Athens who died willingly in battle to fulfill a prophecy.

E   and the more outstanding they are, the more they strive for it, because their love is for immortality. Those who are pregnant in body turn instead to women, and their erotic passion goes in that direction, so that, as they imagine, they might procure immortality and remembrance and happiness for themselves for all the time to come by means of begetting children.

209A   But others are pregnant in soul, for there are indeed people,' she said, 'who experience pregnancy in their souls even more than in their bodies, and they conceive and give birth to things appropriate for a soul to bring forth. And what things are appropriate for it? Wisdom and the rest of virtue, of which all the poets are progenitors, as are all those craftsmen who are spoken of as inventors. But by far the greatest and most beautiful part of practical wisdom is that which has to do with the orderly conduct of cities and households, and which goes by the name of moderation and justice. And when someone

B   who is divinely favored has been pregnant in soul from his youth onward and reaches the prime of life already filled with a desire to give birth and beget offspring, I imagine that he too goes around seeking the beautiful thing in the presence of which he might generate, since he could never generate in the presence of anything ugly. So it is because he is pregnant that he is attracted to beautiful bodies rather than ugly ones, and if by chance he meets up with one who is also beautiful and well-bred and of a good natural disposition in soul, he is utterly enthralled with the combination of the two, and he immediately overflows with speeches to this person about

C   virtue and about the way a good man ought to be and what he ought to devote himself to, and he takes in hand the other's education. For it is my view that by contact with the beautiful one and by close association with him, he gives birth to and brings forth what he has been pregnant with for so long, and whether present or absent the beautiful one fills his mind. And he nurtures what has been generated in common with that beautiful one, so that such people maintain a much closer

communion with each other than that which comes with having children, and a more stable friendship, because the offspring they have in common are more beautiful and more
immortal. Everyone would gladly accept having offspring of
this sort as his own, rather than human children, and would   D
look upon Homer and Hesiod and the other good poets with
envy for the kinds of offspring they left behind them, which
gained them fame and remembrance that are undying, just as
those works themselves are. And, if you don't mind my saying so,'[45] she said, 'these are the sorts of offspring Lycurgus
left behind in Sparta to be the saviors not only of Sparta itself
but even, one might say, of Greece. And among you, Solon is
esteemed for the begetting of your laws, as are other men in   E
many other places, both in Greece and among the barbarians,
for showing forth many beautiful deeds and begetting virtue
in all its manifold array. Many shrines to these men have come
into being before now because of offspring of this sort, but
none yet for anyone because of his human children.

"'Now perhaps even you, Socrates, could be initiated up   210A
to this point into the lore of love, but I do not know whether
you would be capable of the rites and mysteries that are the
ultimate goal of all the rest, if one goes after them in the right
way. I will tell you about them, though,' she said, 'and I will
have no lack of eagerness, so try to follow the best you can.
Because it is necessary,' she said, 'for anyone who goes about
this matter in the right way to begin going toward beautiful
bodies while still young, and first of all, if his guide is guiding him rightly, he must fall in love with one body and generate beautiful speeches in its presence; then he must recognize
that the beauty joined with any particular body is the twin of   B
that which is joined with any other body, and if he needs to

45. Diotima, as a foreigner, apologizes for her praise of Athens's enemy,
Sparta, as though she were saying "no offense meant." The Peloponnesian war
was ongoing at the time of Agathon's dinner party.

pursue what is beautiful in form, it would be exceedingly foolhardy not to regard the beauty joined with all bodies as one
and the same; and with this in mind, he needs to make himself a lover of all beautiful bodies, and slacken his passionate
ardor for one of them, looking down on it and considering it
a trifling thing; after that he must come to regard the beauty
in souls as more to be prized than that in the body, so much
so that even if someone who is decent in soul has only a slight

C   youthful bloom, that is enough to inspire him to be loving and
caring and to give birth to and seek out the sorts of speeches
that will make the young better, so that this quest might com-
pel him to set his sight upon what is beautiful in moral practices and laws and see that all of these are in kinship with one
another,[46] and thus he might regard bodily beauty as being
a trifling thing; and after morality he must be led to con-
templative studies, to set his sight in turn on beauty within

D   these forms of knowledge, gazing now upon a beauty that is
wide-ranging, and no longer that of one particular thing, as if
he were some flunky who is satisfied with the beauty of a little child, or of any human being, or of a single moral practice,
and is servile and small-minded in the way he enslaves himself
to it; he must instead turn to the expansive sea of the beautiful, and by gazing upon it give birth to beauteous and splendid speeches and thoughts in the ungrudging profusion of
philosophy, until, once he has been nourished and fortified in
that activity, he discerns a certain singular knowledge, which

E   is of so great, such intense a beauty as I am about to tell you.

---

46. "Moral practices" translates *epitêdeumata*, and refers to ways of acting acquired by discipline or maintained conscientiously. The kinship among
these may be twofold. A variety of such practices within one society may foster the same underlying virtues, and the variety that exists among places with
differing customs and laws may still have a deeper sameness at its core. In an
example used by Herodotus in III, 38 of his *History*, a shared belief in honoring the dead is codified in two different societies in practices that are mutually
horrifying.

Try to give me your full attention now,' she said, 'the fullest of which you are capable.'

"'Anyone who has been guided up to this point in erotic matters by his tutor, and has taken the kinds of beautiful things in view step by step in the right order, is now approaching the ultimate goal of all erotic striving, and will suddenly come into view of something wondrously beautiful in its nature, and this, Socrates, is the goal for the sake of which all his previous efforts have been made. First of all, it is always in being, never subject to coming into being or passing away, and never increasing or decreasing; next, it is not partly beautiful and partly ugly, or beautiful at one time and not at another, or beautiful in some respect and ugly in some other, or beautiful somewhere and ugly somewhere else, as if it could be beautiful for some and ugly for others; nor again will its beauty make its appearance as a face or hands or anything else that forms part of a body, nor as any formulation or piece of knowledge, nor as being in any way dependent on anything else, such as on some living soul either on earth or in heaven or anywhere else, but being always uniform, itself by itself in virtue of itself, while all other beautiful things partake of it in such a manner that it does not become any greater or less when those other things come into being and pass away, and is not affected in any way. So whenever someone who loves boys in the right way makes the ascent from these particular beauties to that beauty and begins to behold it, the ultimate goal is almost within his grasp. For this is the right way to approach erotic matters, or be led to them by someone else: starting from the beautiful things around us and continually climbing upward for the sake of that beauty, using these beautiful things here as rungs of a ladder, ascending from one to two and from two to all beautiful bodies, and from beautiful bodies to beautiful moral practices, and from moral practices to beautiful understandable things, and from understandable things arriving at last at that act of understanding which is concerned with noth-

211A

B

C

ing else than grasping that very beauty, and finally discerns
the beautiful itself for what it is. And that, my dear Socrates,'
said our Mantinean visitor, 'that, if anywhere, is the state in
which life is worth living for a human being, in contemplation of the beautiful itself. If you ever behold it, it will seem
to you to bear no comparison to gold and finery and beautiful boys and young men, the things that now overwhelm you
so much when you see them that you—you and many others
besides—are ready to look at and be with your beloved ones
forever if that were possible, not eating or drinking but just
gazing at them and being with them. So what do we imagine
would happen,' she said, 'if someone were to look upon the
beautiful itself, unadulterated, pure, undiluted, not contami-
nated with human flesh and its stains and the rest of the vast
litter of mortality? What if he were able to look directly at
divine beauty itself in the unity of its form? Do you imagine,'
she said, 'it would be a shabby sort of life for a human being
to reach that place, looking upon that object with the kind of
sight by which it needs to be contemplated, and being in its
presence? Don't you realize,' she said, 'that it is only in that
place, where he can behold the beautiful with the sight by
which it is visible, that he will attain the ability to give birth
not to phantasms of virtue, since it is no phantasm that is in
his grasp, but to true virtue, since it is the truth that is in his
grasp? True virtue is what he gives birth to and nurtures, and
he will gain for himself the love of the gods; if any human
being has a way of becoming immortal, it is he.'

"And so, Phaedrus and the rest of you, these are the things
Diotima said, and I am persuaded of them. And because I
am persuaded of them, I try to persuade others as well that
no one could easily find a better partner for human nature
in its efforts toward this attainment than Love. And this is
why I assert that every true man ought to pay honor to Love
as I myself honor and practice Love's rites with extraordinary
devotion, and why I encourage others to do the same; and

so, both now and always, I sing the praises of the power and
courage of Love to the greatest extent of my ability. So if you   C
wish, Phaedrus, you may take this speech as an encomium
delivered to Love, or if not, just call it by whatever name you
please."

After Socrates spoke these words, some people indicated
their approval, but Aristophanes was trying to say something,
since Socrates had made mention of his speech in delivering
his own. But then there was a sudden knocking on the courtyard door, and a loud racket coming from a band of revelers, and the sound of a flute-girl could be heard. Agathon said   D
"Why don't you take a look, boys, and if any of our usual circle of friends is there, call him in? If not, say that we're not
drinking and the party is already breaking up."

And not long afterward they heard the voice of Alcibiades
in the courtyard, very drunk and making a noisy fuss, asking
where Agathon was and demanding to be taken to Agathon.
So he was brought in to where they were, with the flute-girl
and some others from his crowd holding him up, and there he
stood in the doorway, crowned with a shaggy wreath of ivy-   E
leaves and violets and decorated with a lot of ribbons all over
his head, and he said, "Greetings, gentlemen. Will you let a
drunken man, a very, very drunken man, drink with you? Or
should we just crown Agathon with a wreath, which is what
we came for, and go away? Because I tell you," he went on,
"I couldn't manage to get anywhere near you yesterday, so I
came here now with these ribbons on my head to wind them
like this off of my head onto the head of the smartest and most
beautiful man—well, what if I do say it! So you're laughing
at me for being drunk? Well you can laugh, but I know per-   213A
fectly well that I'm telling the truth. So tell me on the spot, do
I come in on my terms or not? Will you have a drink with me
or not?"

Then everybody shouted out a raucous welcome and urged
him to come in and lie down on a couch, and Agathon called

him over. And he came in, led along by his people; at the same
time, he was unwinding his ribbons to wreathe them onto
Agathon and had them in front of his eyes so that he didn't
B see Socrates, but sat down beside Agathon, between him and
Socrates, who had made room for him when he saw him coming. So he was sitting next to him as he hugged Agathon and
began wreathing him. Then Agathon said, "Take off Alcibiades' shoes, boys, so he can lie here and make three of us."

And Alcibiades said, "Yes indeed, but who is this third
drinking companion we've got here?" Then turning around
toward him he saw Socrates and as he caught sight of him, he
jumped up and yelled, "Heracles! What's this? Socrates here!
C Lying in wait again to ambush me here the way you're always
doing, suddenly popping up where I imagine you're least likely
to be? What are you doing here now? And why did you lie
down in this spot? Why not next to Aristophanes, or anyone
else who can take a joke and likes that just fine? But no, you
have to manage things so you're lying down at the side of the
most beautiful person in the room."

And Socrates said, "Agathon, see what you can do to protect me. My love for this fellow has turned out to be no laugh-
D ing matter. Ever since the time when I fell in love with him,
I'm no longer allowed to look at or talk to a beautiful man,
not even one, or else this fellow here gets jealous and vin-
dictive toward me and carries on in unbelievable ways, and
heaps abuse on me, and can hardly keep his mitts off me.
So see to it that he doesn't do anything like that now; keep
the peace between us, or if he does attempt violence, protect
me, because I'm utterly terrified of this man's crazed passion
for love."

"No," said Alcibiades, "there's not going to be any peace
between me and you. But I'll put off my revenge on you for
E these things to another time. For now, Agathon," he said, "give
me some of those ribbons so I can garland this wonderful head
of this man, so he won't be able to blame me for crowning

you but then failing to crown him, when he's victorious over all human beings in speeches, not just once the way you were recently but all the time." And as he was speaking, he took some ribbons and garlanded Socrates and then lay down.

Then when he was reclining there, he said, "Look here, gentlemen, you seem sober to me and that's not permissible for you. You've got to drink; that's been settled between us. And to be chairman of our drinking session, I select, until such time as you've caught up on your drinking, myself. So Agathon, if there's a big drinking cup, let it be brought to me— oh, no need, this is better," he said, "bring me that tub, boy," because he saw one that would hold more than half a gallon. And when this was topped up, the first thing he did was drink it down, and then he ordered it refilled for Socrates, and said, "My clever ruse will be no use on Socrates, gentlemen. Notwithstanding the fact that he drinks down as much as anyone presses on him, he never gets drunk." 214A

And Socrates drank it as soon as the boy had poured, but Eryximachus said, "How are we supposed to be doing this, Alcibiades? Do we say nothing over our cups like this, and not even sing a song, but just keep guzzling unceremoniously like people whose throats are parched?" B

"Eryximachus!" said Alcibiades, "superlative son of a superlative and most abstinent father, cheers!"

"The same to you," said Eryximachus, "but what do we do?"

"Whatever you tell us, since you must be obeyed, for 'A man with the art of healing carries as much weight as a multitude of others.'[47] So give us your prescription."

"Listen, then," said Eryximachus. "We decided before you came in that each man in succession from left to right must deliver a speech about Love, singing his praises as beautifully as he could, and all the rest of us have had our say. And C

---

47. *Iliad* XI, 514.

since you haven't spoken, and have drunk up, it's only right for you to give a speech; after you've spoken, you can dictate to Socrates whatever you want him to do, and he to the man on his right, and so on around again."

"What you say is all well and good, Eryximachus," Alcibiades said, "but to match up a drunken man against the speeches of sober ones is not a contest on equal terms. And besides, you blessed innocent, did you believe anything Socrates has just been saying? Don't you know that everything he said is just the other way around? If I praise anyone other than him in his presence, whether it's a god or another human being, *he's* the one who can't keep his mitts off *me*."

"Can't you refrain from blasphemy?" said Socrates.

"By Poseidon, don't even try to object," said Alcibiades, "I could never praise a single other person in your presence."

"Then do it that way if you like," said Eryximachus, "praise Socrates."

"Do you mean it, Eryximachus?" said Alcibiades. "You think I ought to? Shall I really let the man have it and get my revenge right in front of you fellows?"

"Hey, now," said Socrates, "what have you got in mind? Turning me into a laughingstock with your praises? Or what are you going to do?"

"I'm just going to tell the truth, if you see fit to allow it."

"By all means," he said, "you have not only my permission but my insistence that you tell the truth."

"No sooner said than done," said Alcibiades, "and here's what you can do. If I say anything that's not true, please stop me right in the midst of it and say that I'm lying about that. Because there's nothing that I'll be intentionally lying about. But if I get one thing mixed up with another in my recollections, you shouldn't be surprised, since it's no easy matter for someone in my condition to give a fluent and orderly account of your eccentricity."

D

F

215A

Alcibiades' Speech

"Gentlemen, my way of taking on the praise of Socrates will be through images.[48] *He* will probably think I'm doing this to make him a laughingstock, but the purpose of the image is not laughter but truth. Because I claim that he most closely resembles those Silenus-statues you can find sitting in the shops where the Herms are sold; the Sileni are the ones the craftsmen carve as holding pipes or flutes, and when they're taken apart in two halves they're revealed as having little figures of gods inside. And I claim that he also resembles the satyr Marsyas. As far as looks go at any rate, Socrates, I don't suppose you yourself would dispute that you resemble them, but you're like them in every other way too; just listen. You're an arrogant man,[49] aren't you? If you won't admit it, I can produce witnesses. And a flute-player too? A far more wonderful one than Marsyas. He used to entrance human beings by means of instruments with the power from his lips, and so does anyone who plays his music even now—for I say it was

B

C

48. Alcibiades draws on a cluster of images. The satyrs were wild spirits who inhabited wooded and mountainous regions, semi-human in form, with strong appetites for wine, sex, and frenzied music. The Sileni were older and perhaps more civilized versions of these spirits, and Silenus himself was the tutor of the god Dionysus. Marsyas was a satyr who taught the musician Olympus to play the flute; Marsyas himself was skinned alive for presuming to challenge Apollo to a competition on the flute. The figures of Silenus and Marsyas do bear a close facial resemblance to the statues we have of Socrates. The Herms or Hermae which Alcibiades mentions in passing were guardian deities, represented all over Athens, on private and public ground, by vertical stone plinths with heads (usually of Hermes) on top and male genitals on the lower front. The year following that of the dialogue, Alcibiades was accused of being involved in vandalizing the Hermae, and fled to Sparta (in wartime) to escape a death-sentence in Athens. See Thucydides, *Peloponnesian War*, VI, 15, 27–29, 60–61.

49. The word is *hubristês*. It is applied playfully to Socrates by Agathon in 175E; see the note to 181C. Marsyas was guilty of *hubris* toward the gods in the sense that has become common in English, but Alcibiades applies the word to Socrates for treating his charms with indifference (217E, 219C).

Marsyas's music that Olympus used to play after he taught
it to him. So when anyone plays Olympus's melodies on the
flute, whether it's a flute-virtuoso or some lowly flute-girl, it
is these melodies alone that cause people to be possessed and
show who is open to receive the gods and the rites of initiation, because the music itself is of divine origin. And you differ from Marsyas to this extent only, that you do this same

D   thing without instruments in plain, unadorned speech. When
we listen to anyone else delivering other sorts of speeches anyway, and it may be a thoroughly accomplished orator, one
might say no one cares a bit. But whenever anyone listens
to you, or to someone else telling things you've said, even if
the one doing the telling is an utterly incompetent speaker,
no matter whether the one listening is man, woman, or child,
we're bowled over and we become possessed. In my case at
any rate, gentlemen, if it wouldn't make me appear utterly and
totally inebriated, I would have sworn to you on my oath what
I've experienced first-hand from this man's words, and what

E   I'm still experiencing even now. Whenever I listen to him, I'm
much worse off than the frenzied Corybantic priests, the way
my heart pounds and my tears flow in response to this man's
words, and I see lots and lots of other people having the same
reaction. When I used to listen to Pericles and other good ora-
tors, I'd judge them to be speaking excellently, but I've never
had an experience like *that*, throwing my soul into turmoil
and casting me down into abject misery as bad as any slave's,
but in response to this Marsyas sitting here, time and time

216A   again I've been reduced to such a state that it seemed to me
life wasn't worth living for someone in my condition. And
you, Socrates, can't deny that this is the truth. Even now, I'm
fully aware that if I lent him my ears I could by no means
resist, but would suffer the same way. Because he forces me to
admit that I have serious faults, and yet I continue to neglect
myself while I'm so busy with Athenian politics. So in self-de-
fense, I stop up my ears as though against the Sirens, and run

away to avoid sitting there at his side until I get old and gray. And there is something that happens to me in the presence of this man alone out of all human beings, something which no one would ever expect to find in me, that anyone could make me feel ashamed. But I do feel ashamed around him and him alone. I'm well aware that I don't have a leg to stand on to argue that I don't need to do what he tells me, but as soon as I get away from him, my head is turned by the flattery of the crowd. I sneak off and run away from him, and when I see him again, the things he's made me admit fill me with shame. Often, I'd gladly see him blotted out of the human world, but then again, if this were to happen, I know perfectly well that would make me much more miserable, so I have no idea what I can do about this fellow.

"So that's the experience I and lots of others have had with the flute-music this satyr plays. But hear me out about the other ways he resembles the figures I've likened him to, and how wondrous a power he has. Because mark my words, not a one of you knows this man. But now that I've gotten started, I'm going to expose him. What you see is a man who's erotically inclined toward beautiful young men, always hanging around them and smitten with them, and who's also ignorant of everything and doesn't know a thing—that's the role he's playing. And isn't that just like a Silenus? Absolutely. He wears this guise on the outside, the same way a Silenus is formed by a sculptor. But do you realize, gentlemen and drinking companions, how full he is on the inside once he's opened up—how full of temperance? You can take it from me that it doesn't make a bit of difference to him if anyone is beautiful; he has so much disdain for it that one could hardly imagine it, and the same is true if someone is rich or has any other distinction that most people look on as happiness. He regards all these goods as worthless, and us who have them as worthless too— I'm telling you! He spends his whole life being ironic and playing with people. I don't know if any of you have caught him

when he's being serious and open, and discovered the treas-
ures inside, but I saw them once, and they seemed to me to be

so divine and golden and supremely beautiful and wondrous
that, well, one simply had to do what Socrates said. And since
I believed he was seriously taken with my youthful beauty, I
thought this was a godsend and an amazing stroke of luck for
me, and that I had the opportunity, by gratifying Socrates, to
hear everything that he knew, because I was amazingly vain
about my youthful beauty. Now before this I had been in the
habit of never being with him alone, without an attendant, but

with my plan in mind, I dismissed the attendant one day, and
did get together with him alone—well, I have to tell you gentlemen the whole truth. Just pay attention, and if I tell a lie,
Socrates, you call me out on it. So, gentlemen, I got together
with him one on one, and I imagined he would immediately
start talking to me the way a lover talks to his beloved in private, and I was thrilled. But nothing like that happened at
all; he spent the day with me in our usual sort of conversa-

tion, then went off and left. So after that I invited him to go
to the gym with me, and I exercised with him, thinking that
would get the job done on the spot. But he exercised with me,
and even wrestled with me several times with no one around,
and do I have to say it? I got nothing more out of it. When I
accomplished nothing by any of that, I decided that a full-
scale attack had to be made on the man. I couldn't give up
once I'd taken up the challenge, and I had to find out once
and for all what was the matter. So I invited him to have dinner with me, exactly as if I were the lover scheming to con-

quer his beloved. And he wasn't even quick to accept that from
me, though he was persuaded eventually. But the first time he
came, he wanted to leave after he had eaten, and that time I
was so embarrassed I let him go. So the next time I had a plan,
and after we had eaten I kept the conversation going with him
without pause far into the night, and when he wanted to leave,
I used the fact that it was late as an excuse, and insisted on his

staying. So he settled back on the couch next to mine where he'd had dinner, and no one else was sleeping in the room except the two of us. Now up to this point in my story, it would be perfectly acceptable to tell it in the presence of anyone, but you wouldn't hear me say any more from here on, except that, in the first place, there's the saying that wine, with or without the 'mouths of babes' part, is always truthful, and secondly, it seems to me to be unfair, once I've embarked on the praise of Socrates, to keep you in the dark about his act of splendid arrogance. And besides, I'm in the same condition as someone who's snakebit. They say that anyone who's had this experience is unwilling to talk about what it's like except to those who've been bitten, since they're the only ones who'd understand him and make allowances for anything he may have been driven by his torments to do and say. Well I've been bitten by a more painful snake and in the most painful place anyone could be bitten, because I've felt the strike and the sting of the speeches involved in philosophy in my heart or soul or whatever one should call it, and they have a more ferocious grip than any viper when they get hold of a young soul that's not without natural ability, and there's no limit to what they can make it do and say. I'm looking around at Phaedruses, Agathons, Eryximachuses, Pausaniases, Aristophaneses—Socrates himself, it goes without saying—and all the rest, every one of whom has had his share of the madness and frenzy of philosophy, so every one of you will hear it, since you can make allowances for what was done then and what is said now. But as for the house-servants, and anyone else who is uninitiated and unrefined, you'll have to shut your ears with great big doors.

"All right then, gentlemen, the lamp had been put out and the servants were out of the room, and I decided that there was no need to mince words with him, and I'd just tell him frankly what I had in mind. So I nudged him and said, 'Socrates, are you asleep?'

E

218A

B

C

"'Not at all,' he said.

"'Do you know what I've decided?'

"'What in particular?' he said.

"And I said, 'You seem to me to be the only worthy person among my lovers, and yet you appear to be hesitant to say anything to me about it. Well, here's the way I feel: I think it would be downright stupid for me not to gratify you in this matter and with anything else you might need from either my property or my friends. For nothing is more important to me than becoming the most excellent man I can be, and I can't imagine that there is anyone better able to be my partner in this effort than you. I'd be much more ashamed in front of sensible people for *not* gratifying such a man than I'd be in front of the masses of fools *for* gratifying him.'

D

"And when he'd heard this, he, in that very ironic manner that is so habitual with him and so much his own, said, 'My dear Alcibiades, there may be hope for you yet if what you say about me happens to be true, and there is some power in me that could help you become a better man. That's surely some inconceivable beauty you see in me if it greatly surpasses your own beauty of form. So if, having noticed this, you're trying to make a deal with me and barter beauty for beauty, that's no small swindle you're looking to pull off on me; you're attempting to get the true in return for the apparent in the realm of beauties, so what you really have in mind is an exchange of 'gold for bronze.'[50] But consider it better, you blessed innocent, in case you're failing to notice that I'm not worth anything. Certainly the vision of the understanding only begins to see things sharply when that of the eyes is starting to pass its prime, and you're still far from that.'

E

219A

"When I heard this, I said 'My position has been stated,

---

50. *Iliad* VI, 235–236. This became a proverb, like trading a cow for a handful of beans, but it is less often noticed that in Bk. II, lines 872–875 of the *Iliad*, Homer alerts his audience to the fact that for armor, gold is not better than bronze.

and not a word of it differs from what I think. It's up to you to determine what you judge to be best for you and me.'

"'Well,' he said, 'you've got that part right at least, and in the days ahead we'll do whatever seems best, upon reflection, to the two of us together, about these things and everything else.'

"After I'd said and heard these things, I felt as though I'd fired off my arrows and he'd been hit. So without giving him a chance to say anything more, I got up and covered him with my cloak—since it was wintertime—and I snuggled in under the light wrap that's all this fellow wears, and put my two arms around this true and wondrous inhabitant of the spirit world, and lay there the whole night through. And you, Socrates, can't say I'm lying about any of these things either. But when I'd done all that, this man remained so aloof, so disdainful, so derisive of my youthful charm, and so humiliatingly arrogant about it—and on that score I thought I was really something, gentlemen of the jury—that's right, you are jurymen trying Socrates on a charge of aggravated arrogance—and here's the point: before all the gods and goddesses, you can be fully assured that when I got up, I had not slept with Socrates in any sense beyond that in which I might have spent the night with a father or older brother.

"Just imagine what state of mind I was in after that, feeling insulted but full of admiration for this man's nature, with its temperance and fortitude; I had met up with a human being of a sort I would never have expected to encounter, with such wise judgment and such strength of character. There was no way I was going to hold a grudge and deprive myself of this man's company, but I had no resources by which I could win him over to me. I knew perfectly well that he was far more invulnerable on all sides to money than Ajax was to iron,[51] and in the only way I thought I could make a conquest of

B

C

D

E

---

51. Ajax, son of Telamon, carried an exceptionally tall and thick shield in battle at Troy (*Iliad* VII, 206–223).

him, he had escaped me. So I was at a loss, drifting along enslaved to this human being as no one has ever been enslaved to anyone else. Now it was after all this had happened to me that we went together on the military campaign to Potidaea, and we were messmates there, and in the first place, he surpassed not only me but also everyone else in the midst of hardships; whenever we were cut off somewhere and forced, the way one is on campaigns, to go hungry, the rest of us were nothing compared to him when it came to endurance. And then in turn at times when there were plentiful supplies, he was the only one able to take full advantage of them, especially because he didn't really want to drink, but when pressed to, he outdid us all, and what was most awe-inspiring of all, no human being ever saw Socrates drunk. I'd say this will be put to the test again presently. But it was in connection with endurance of the winter—and winters up there are horrendous—that he performed amazing feats, especially one time when there was one of those coatings of ice that are the most daunting of all, and everybody either didn't stir from inside the tents or, if any did go out, they were bundled up in an amazing number of layers and with their feet wrapped in felt and sheepskins over their shoes, but this man went outside in these conditions in just the sort of cloak he'd been accustomed to wear before, and he made his way barefoot over the ice more easily than the rest of us did with shoes on, while the soldiers gave him dirty looks, thinking he was doing it to show them up.

220A

B

C

"That's enough about that, 'but what an amazing thing this stalwart man had the mettle to do'[52] on the campaign there one day is worth hearing. He became immersed in thought about something at dawn and stood in one spot pondering it, and when he couldn't resolve it, he didn't let it go but stood there pursuing it. It was already midday when peo-

52. *Odyssey* IV, 242.

ple started to take notice, and one would remark to another in wonder that Socrates had been standing there thinking about something since early morning. Finally, when it was evening, some of the Ionian soldiers, after they'd finished dinner—this time it was summer—brought their sleeping mats outside, partly so they could lie down in the cool air but also in order to watch and see if he would keep standing there all night as well. And he did keep standing there until dawn arrived and the sun rose, and after offering a prayer to the sun, he went off and left.

D

"And then, if you like, there's what he did in the battles, and justice requires me to give him his due for that, because when the battle took place for which the generals gave *me* the award for bravery, it was this man, and no other human being besides, who saved my life. He was unwilling to abandon me when I was wounded, but pitched in and not only saved me but kept me from losing my weapons. I urged the generals at the time to give the award to you, Socrates, and you can't find fault with me on that score or say that I'm lying about it. But when the generals, with their eyes on my social prominence, wanted to give the award to me, you were more eager than they were that I should get it rather than yourself. And also on this theme, gentlemen, Socrates was a sight worth seeing when our army was making its retreat from Delium. I happened to be beside him on horseback while he was in armor in the infantry. So while the men were already scattering in all directions, he was retreating along with Laches when I came across them, and as soon as I saw the pair of them, I encouraged them to take heart and told them I wouldn't abandon them. So I had a more beautiful view of Socrates there than at Potidaea, since I had less to worry about for myself as a result of being on horseback. First of all, I saw how much more cool and collected he was than Laches. Then too, it seemed to me, Aristophanes, that your phrase applied, and that he was strolling along there the way he does here at home, 'with his head

E

221A

B

held high and his eyes cast wide,'[53] calmly glancing from side to side at friends and enemies alike, making it crystal clear to everyone, even from a long way off, that if anyone laid a hand on this man, he'd put up a robust defense. And that was what allowed both him and his comrade to get away safely, since people hardly ever bother those who bear themselves that way

C   in war; they chase down the ones who are running off in head-long flight.

"Now there are many other wondrous things one could praise Socrates for, and among those other characteristics of his one might speak of them in relation to some other person as well, but what is worthy of absolute wonder is the way he is like no other human being who ever lived, in ancient times or the present day. One might liken the sort of person Achilles was to Brasidas and others, and the sort Pericles was to Nestor

D   and Antenor—and there are others; and in the same way one might find a likeness for all the rest. But the sort of person this fellow here is, when it comes to eccentricity, in himself and in his talk, no one could come near finding no matter how much he looked, among those of today or those of the distant past, unless one were to liken him to the counterparts I've spoken of, not any human being at all but silenuses and satyrs, and that applies not only to him but to his talk as well.

"Now here's something I left out in my first remarks, that his talk is exactly like those silenuses that can be opened up.

E   For if anyone cares to listen to the things Socrates says, his first impression would be that they're completely ridiculous. The sort of words and phrases that they're all wrapped up in on the outside are just the hide of some uncouth[54] satyr. He talks

---

53. *Clouds* 362. Socrates had bulging eyes that widened his peripheral vision; see Xenophon's *Symposium*, V, 5.

54. The word is *hubristês* again, here perhaps close to the sense in which Pausanias used it in 181C, for someone who flouts the sensibilities of polite society. The verb from the same root is used one last time just below, where it is translated "treat with scorn."

about jackasses bearing burdens and about blacksmiths and shoemakers and tanners, and he always seems to be repeating the same things with the same examples, so any random person with no experience and no sense would laugh at the things he says. But when they're opened up and someone gets inside them and sees what's there, the first thing he'll discover is that they're the only speeches that have any sense in them, and the next thing is that they're the most godlike words one could ever hear, that they have in them the most splendid images of virtue, that they are the most far-reaching, indeed all-encompassing, of the proper studies for someone who is intent upon being splendid and excellent.[55]

222A

"These, gentlemen, are the things I have to say in praise of Socrates; and to mix in the things I blame him for, I told you how he treated me with scorn. I am not, however, the only one he has treated that way; Charmides, the son of Glaucon, and Euthydemus, the son of Diocles, and very many others have been deceived by this man, who presents himself as a lover while he makes himself the beloved instead of the lover. I'm saying this for your benefit, Agathon, so you don't fall for his deception but learn from our experience to be wary, and you won't have to learn it the hard way like the proverbial dunce."

B

When Alcibiades said these things, there was some laughter at his frankness, because it showed that he was still in love with Socrates.

C

Then Socrates said, "You seem sober to me, Alcibiades. Otherwise you could never have surrounded yourself with such an ingenious smokescreen to try to hide the real reason you were saying all these things, and slip it in at the end of your speech as if it were an afterthought. Your purpose was to cause discord between Agathon and me because you think I

D

55. "Splendid and excellent" translates *kalos kagathos*, the phrase used by the Athenian upper classes for their own superiority. See the note to 204A, where Diotima uses the phrase in speaking of the sort of self-satisfaction that makes people incapable of desiring the good things they lack.

ought to love no one but you and Agathon ought to be loved by no one but you. But you didn't get away with it; this satyr-play[56] of yours, or silenus-play, has been exposed. My dear Agathon, don't let him be successful, but see to it that no one causes any discord between you and me."

E

Then Agathon said, "What you're saying may very well be the truth, Socrates. My evidence is the fact that he sat himself down between you and me to split us up. But he won't be successful at all; I'm coming over to lie next to you."

"By all means," said Socrates, "lie down at the end on the other side of me."

"Zeus!" said Alcibiades. "What I have to put up with from this fellow! He thinks he has to get the better of me in every way. At the very least, you extraordinary man, let Agathon lie between us."

"That's impossible," said Socrates, "because you've praised me and I'm supposed to go next and praise the person on my right. So if Agathon is lying next beyond you, doesn't that mean I'd have to be praised again by him before he can be

223A

praised by me? Just leave him alone, you unbelievable man, and don't begrudge the youngster the praise he'll get from me."

"Oh boy, oh boy!" said Agathon. "There's no way I could stay here now, Alcibiades. Nothing can stop me from moving over so I can get praised by Socrates."

"Well that's that, as usual," said Alcibiades. "When Socrates is around, it's impossible for anyone else to get any attention from the beautiful ones. What a resourceful and plausible argument he came up with this time to get this one lying next to him."

B

Then as Agathon was getting up to lie down next to Socrates, an enormous crowd of revelers suddenly showed up at

56. Satyr plays were shorter performances, written by the tragic poets to be presented after tragedies as bawdy comic relief, with a chorus of satyrs and silenuses. Euripides' *Cyclops* is the only complete surviving example.

the door, which they happened to find open for someone who was going out. So they barged straight in among the guests and sat down, and everything was full of noisy confusion; with no sort of order any more, they were obliged to drink voluminous quantities of wine. Then Eryximachus and Phaedrus and some others got up and left, according to what Aristodemus said, and he himself fell asleep and slept for a very long time,   C for the nights were long at the time. He was awakened near daybreak by the crowing of the roosters, and when he woke up he saw that all the others were either asleep or gone, except for Agathon, Aristophanes, and Socrates; they were the only ones still awake, and they were drinking out of a big bowl they were passing from left to right. Socrates was going through a dialectical discussion with them; Aristodemus said he couldn't   D remember the rest of what was said, since he hadn't been there from the beginning and he was still half-asleep, but he said the gist of it was that Socrates was forcing them to admit that it was possible for the same man to have the knowledge to compose comedy and tragedy, and that someone who was a tragic poet by art could also be a comic poet. While they were being forced to this conclusion, they were nodding off and barely following what was said, and Aristophanes was the first to fall asleep, and then just as day was dawning Agathon too. So Socrates, after he'd settled them comfortably, got up and left, with Aristodemus himself following as usual, and when he got to the Lyceum he washed himself up and spent the day the same way as any other, and having spent it that way, took his own rest at home that evening.

PHAEDRUS

SOCRATES Phaedrus, dear friend, where are you headed and where   227A
are you coming from?

PHAEDRUS From Lysias, son of Cephalus, Socrates, and I'm on my
way outside the walls for a walk, because I spent a long time
with him, sitting down since early morning. I'm taking the
advice of your friend and mine, Acumenus, and taking my
walk on the country roads, since he says exercise there is more
refreshing than in the cloistered walkways.   B

SOCRATES And that was good advice, my friend. So Lysias, it
seems, was in town?

PHAEDRUS Yes, at Epicrates' place near the temple of Olympian
Zeus, the house Morychus used to own.

SOCRATES And what was the topic of discourse? Clearly, Lysias
must have been regaling you all with speeches.

PHAEDRUS Listen and learn as you walk along, if you're at leisure
from any pressing business.

SOCRATES What? Don't you realize hearing your discussion with
Lysias would have "a higher claim than any business" on me,
in Pindar's words?

PHAEDRUS Lead on.   C

SOCRATES And speak on, please.

PHAEDRUS And really, Socrates, you're just the right person to
hear it, because the speech that we talked about had to do
with love, though I don't know quite how to put it. For Lysias
has described someone attempting a seduction of one of the

119

beauties, but not by a lover—and that's just what's so exquisite about it; he says that it's the non-lover who ought to be gratified rather than the lover.

SOCRATES Oh, how magnanimous! I wish he'd write that it ought to be someone poor rather than rich, old rather than young, and all the other attributes that belong to me and to most of us. Then his speeches would not only be urbane but public-spirited, too. Now my heart is so set on hearing you that I won't leave you even if you take your walk all the way to Megara, and right back again after you get to the wall, the way Herodicus recommends.

PHAEDRUS What do you mean, Socrates, you remarkable fellow? Are you assuming that I, a mere amateur in these matters, can recall in a manner worthy of Lysias things that he, the most formidable man now writing, composed at his leisure over a long time? Far from it, even though I'd rather have that ability than a fortune in money.

SOCRATES Oh, Phaedrus! If I don't know Phaedrus, I've forgotten myself. But neither of these things is true, and I'm quite sure that when the man I know listened to Lysias's speech he didn't just hear it once but insisted that he repeat what he'd said over and over, and that the other was more than happy to oblige. But not even that satisfied the man I know, and he ended up by getting the written speech and looking over the parts that captivated him most, which he sat there doing from early morning until he got tired and went for a walk. And by the dog,[1] I do believe he's learned the whole speech by heart,

D

228A

B

---

1. This oath, used frequently by Socrates in Plato's dialogues, is rarely found anywhere else. In the *Gorgias* (482B), Socrates makes it evident that the dog is Anubis, an Egyptian deity corresponding to the Greek Hermes. In *The Music of the Republic* (Paul Dry Books, 2004, pp. 118–119), Eva Brann interprets the oath as an invocation of divine aid for the labor of self-examination. In the passage cited from the *Gorgias*, Socrates appeals to Callicles to reflect on a contradiction deep within himself. Here, it seems to be Phaedrus's infatuation with other people's writings that is standing in the way of his knowing himself. See 229E below.

unless it's a very long one, and he's going outside the walls to practice it. But lo and behold, he meets up with someone who has a lovesick passion for hearing speeches, and, delighted to have a partner in his raptures, he tells him to lead on. But when the lover of speeches begged him to speak, he put on a show of being coy, as if he weren't just dying to speak, but he was determined to end up speaking regardless, even if no one was willing to listen. So you beg him, Phaedrus, to do this moment without more ado what he's going to do soon anyway.

C

PHAEDRUS Well, truly, it's much the best thing for me to speak however I'm able, since I can't see any way you're going to let me off until I do speak one way or another.

SOCRATES Your impression of me is exactly right.

PHAEDRUS Here's how I'll go about it, then, for really and truly, Socrates, I haven't learned the words by heart. But I can go through the rough sense of all the ways in which he said the situation of the lover is superior to that of the non-lover, taking up each point in summary and in order, beginning with the first.

D

SOCRATES Yes, dear friend, after you've first shown me what you have in your left hand, under your cloak. For my guess is you've got the speech itself. And if that's true, you can take it from me that even though I love you dearly, I'm not about to offer myself to you to practice on when Lysias is right here. So come on, show me.

E

PHAEDRUS Enough. You've dashed the hope I had of going through my paces on you, Socrates. But where do you want us to sit down and read?

SOCRATES Let's turn aside here and go down by the Ilissus; then we can sit quietly wherever we like.

229A

PHAEDRUS I'm in luck, as it seems, since I happen to be barefoot. You, of course, always are. That makes it easiest for us to go wading along the stream, which won't be unpleasant, especially at this season of the year and time of day.

SOCRATES Lead on, and look out for a place for us to sit.

PHAEDRUS Do you see that lofty plane tree?[2]

SOCRATES What about it?

B PHAEDRUS There's shade there, and a gentle breeze, and grass to sit on, or lie on if we want to.

SOCRATES Lead on, please.

PHAEDRUS Tell me, Socrates, isn't it from along here by the Ilissus that Boreas is said to have carried off Oreithyia?

SOCRATES That is what's said.

PHAEDRUS From right here maybe? The stream looks charming and pure and clear, a perfect place for girls to play beside.

C SOCRATES No, it's as much as a quarter mile or so farther up, where we cross over for the Agra district. That's where there's an altar of Boreas.

PHAEDRUS I've never really noticed it. But by Zeus, Socrates, do you put any credit in this myth as being true?

SOCRATES I wouldn't be exceptional if I disbelieved it, the way the intellectuals do; then I could give the story a pedantic twist and say that a gust of the north wind knocked her off the nearby rocks while she was playing with Pharmacea, and when she'd died that way, people said she'd been snatched

D away by Boreas.[3] But as for me, Phaedrus, while I regard such explanations as charming enough in other respects, I consider them the mark of a man who's overly clever and industrious, but not particularly fortunate, if for no other reason than because he's got to go on after that and correct the figure[4] of

---

2. The name of the species of tree (*platonos*) is a pun on the name of Plato (*Platôn*), which is actually a nickname meaning something like "broad-shouldered." The image stands as a vivid reminder to us, the readers, through everything that follows, of the overarching presence of the dialogue's author.

3. In the manuscripts, the sentence goes on "or else from the Areopagus, since the story is also told this way, that she was snatched away from there and not here." Many editors reject these words as a gloss that crept into the text.

4. The word "figure" here translates *eidos*, the look of anything. The Greek word is used extensively by Plato to refer to the invisible look we always have

the Centaurs, and that of the Chimaera next, and then here comes flooding in a whole throng of such things as Gorgons and Pegasuses and a plethora of other impossibilities as well   E as fantastical monsters composed of diverse natures. If someone who disbelieves in these is going to bring each of them into line with probability, as if consulting some rustic source of wisdom, he'll need a lot of leisure. But I have no leisure at all for that. And the reason for that, my dear friend, is this: I am not yet able, in accordance with the inscription at Delphi, to know myself, and it seems absurd to me to inquire into   230A extraneous matters while I'm still in ignorance about that. So that's why I leave those things alone and accept the traditional opinion about them, while I make my inquiries, as I was saying just now, not into those things but into myself, to learn whether I happen to be a beast more composite and more raging than Typhon⁵ or a tamer and simpler animal that is destined by nature to a divine and modest lot in life. But, my friend, in the midst of our talk, isn't this the tree you were leading us to?

PHAEDRUS The very one.   B

SOCRATES By Hera, what a beautiful spot to rest in! This plane tree is so wide-spreading and lofty, and the willow, with its height and deep shade, is absolutely lovely, at the peak of its bloom too, which gives the place a sweet fragrance; and the

---

an inner eye on when we speak of even the most commonplace things, such as a bee (*Meno* 72A–C) or a weaver's shuttle (*Cratylus* 389A–B). The figures that the rationalist pedant must "correct" are those of the fabulous composite beings that populate myths, including the horse-men, lion-goats, snake-haired maidens, and winged horses mentioned here. Socrates himself will add a memorable figure to this gallery, beginning at 246A below, in an attempt to capture the look of the human soul.

5. According to Hesiod (*Theogony* 823–835), Typhon was a monster who breathed fire through a hundred dragon-heads while roaring, bellowing, and hissing.

stream flowing under the plane tree is utterly charming, and its water is quite cool, as my foot can attest. And it appears, from the statuettes and images, to be a sacred place of some

C   nymphs and of Achelous. Then too, if you please, the air in this spot is filled with soothing and very sweet breezes, and resonant with the mellifluous summery chorus of the cicadas. But the most exquisite refinement of all is the grass that grows thickly enough on the gentle slope that it's perfect to lay one's head on. So, my dear Phaedrus, you've done a first-rate job as a guide.

PHAEDRUS And you, you amazing man, really come across as the most extraordinary person. For you appear to be literally what

D   you say, a foreigner with a guide, and not a local. You don't stray from the city out into the lands beyond the borders, and you don't even seem to me to go outside the walls at all.

SOCRATES You'll have to make allowances for me, you excellent man, because I'm a lover of learning. The fields and trees aren't willing to teach me anything, but the people in the city are. You, however, seem to me to have found the formula to get me out. The same way people lead hungry animals by waving a branch or some fruit in front of them, you dangle speeches on

E   papyrus rolls[6] in front of me and it seems you can lead me all over Attica and anywhere else you please. But now that I'm at this spot, I fully intend to lie down for the time being, while you take up whatever position you think will let you read most comfortably, and read.

PHAEDRUS Listen, then:

"You know my situation, and you've heard what I think is the advantageous way for us to handle these things. And

231A   I don't think I deserve to be denied this request of mine just because I don't happen to be in love with you. For lov-

---

6. What Phaedrus had hidden up his sleeve was a *biblion*, a scroll or "book" in the sense in which the *Republic* was contained on ten books.

ers have second thoughts about the benefits they confer at the time when their desires come to an end, but no such occasion arises for non-lovers to change their minds. For they confer all the benefits in their power, not under the pressure of necessity but willingly, in the way that they determine to be in their own best interests. Furthermore, lovers look at the ways they've managed their own affairs badly on account of their love, along with the benefits they've conferred, and when they add in the trouble they've been put to, they believe they've B long since repaid the favor to those they love at full value. But non-lovers can't use the excuse of neglecting their own affairs for this, or put their past troubles into the accounting, or shift the blame onto quarrels with their relatives. So once so many evils have been eliminated, all that's left for them to do is devote themselves eagerly to whatever actions they think will make their beloveds happy. Furthermore, if it's worth giving great credit to lovers because they claim to treat those whom C they're in love with as their best friends, and to be ready, in order to please their beloveds, to expose themselves to the hatred of others as shown in both words and deeds, it's easy to infer that if they're telling the truth, they'll make a bigger fuss over those they fall in love with later than over their present beloveds, whom they will obviously treat badly if that's what the new ones want. How reasonable is it anyway to turn over such a matter to someone in the grip of such a misfor- D tune, which no one with any experience would even attempt to talk him out of? They themselves even admit that they're sick rather than in their right minds, and that they know their judgment is faulty but are unable to control themselves. So how could they, once their good judgment has been restored, consider the decisions they made while in that condition to be sound ones? Also, if you were to choose the best one from among your lovers, your selection would be made from a small group, but it would be made from a large group if you chose

the person who suits you best from among all the others. So
the hope of hitting upon someone worthy of your friendship is
much greater among so many.

"Now if it's public opinion you're afraid of, and you think
it will be a disgrace to you if people find out about it, the likelihood is that lovers, believing that others are as envious of
them as they are of others, will puff themselves up by talking about it, with a competitive desire to show off to everyone
that they haven't gone to all that trouble for nothing, whereas
the non-lovers are in control of themselves, and will choose
what is best in preference to a reputation people give them.
Furthermore, it's inevitable that many people will hear about
and see the lovers following their beloveds around and making
that their business, so that whenever they're seen engaged in
any exchange of conversation, people will assume that they're
together as a result of some desire, consummated or intended
to be so, whereas people wouldn't even think of finding fault
with non-lovers for being together, knowing that it's necessary
to converse with someone, out of friendship or for some other
pleasure. And if a fear occurs to you when you reflect that it's
difficult for a friendship to be lasting, and though in other
circumstances any falling-out that happens brings a common
misfortune to both parties, once you've given up what matters
most to you it comes as a great injury to you, then it would
reasonably be lovers you should fear more. For many things
are sources of offense to them, and they take everything that
happens as meant to injure them. For that reason they prevent
associations between their beloveds and other men, afraid of
the ones who have wealth because they might outspend them
with their money, and the ones who have educations because
they might be their superiors in intelligence, and they're on
their guard against the influence of anyone who possesses anything good. And if they persuade you to be cut off from all
these, they leave you with a complete absence of friends, but

if you look out for yourself and use better judgment than they do, you'll end up falling out with *them*. On the other hand, all those who happen to be non-lovers, but have attained what they asked for as a consequence of merit, would not be jealous of those who associated with you; instead they would feel hatred for those who were unwilling to do so, considering themselves to be slighted by the latter but benefitted by the attentions of the others. So there is a much greater hope that   E friendship rather than animosity will result from your affair with them.

"Then too, most lovers desire your body before they know your character and become acquainted with the rest of your connections, so that they have no way of knowing whether they'll still want to be friends when their desires have come to an end, whereas with non-lovers who were friends with each   233A other before they did these deeds, it's not likely that these benefits they've received will make their friendship be any less; instead, they will be left behind as reminders of things to come. And then too, you'll be better off being persuaded by me than by a lover. They'll praise whatever you say and do even when those things are not for the best, partly from fear of offending you and partly because their judgment is worse   B as a result of their desire. For these are the ways Love flaunts his power: he makes those who are unlucky in love feel miserable about things that would cause no distress to anyone else, but when they are fortunate, he forces them to give their approval to things that are not even worthy of taking pleasure in; hence it is much more appropriate for those they love to pity them than to hold them in esteem. But if you're persuaded by me, my primary concern in associating with you will not be for present pleasure but for benefit that is to come,   C since I am not overpowered by love but in control of myself, and not prone to take up violent hostility over small matters, but rather to let slight anger build up slowly over large matters, showing forbearance for unintentional wrongs and trying to prevent intentional ones. For these are the signs of a friendship that will last a long time. But if, after all, you can't shake the feeling that strong affection is not possible unless one happens to be in love, you ought to think hard about the fact that then we could not care so much for our sons or our fathers and mothers or have any faithful friends who became attached to us not through that sort of desire but through pursuits of a different sort.

D

"Furthermore, if one ought to gratify those who beg for it the most intensely, it would also be appropriate in other situations to bestow favors not on the best recipients but on the most needy. For since they will be relieved of the greatest hardships, they will also have the most gratitude. So then it would also be right when you have lavish private dinners not to invite your friends but beggars and those in need of a filling meal, for they will be devoted to you and follow you around and hang around your doors and get the most pleasure out of it; their gratitude will not be the smallest and the blessings their prayers will call down upon you will be many. But perhaps it's appropriate to gratify not those with the strongest need but those best able to repay the favor, and not those who just beg for it but those who are worthy of the deed, and not those who will enjoy the bloom of youth in you but those will share the goods they possess with you as you grow older, and not those who will feel competitive with others about their successes but those who will maintain a modest silence with everyone, and not those who will be ardent for a short time but those who will be your constant friends throughout your whole life, and not those who will look for an excuse for hostility once their desire has come to an end, but those who will display their own virtue once the bloom of youth is off you. So you should keep the things I've said in mind, and think hard about the fact that lovers are warned by their friends that their conduct is harmful, but none of their relatives ever found fault with

E

234A

B

non-lovers for making bad decisions about their own interests on that account.

"Now perhaps you will ask me whether I'm advising you to gratify all non-lovers. Well, I don't suppose the lover will urge you to steer your thinking in that direction toward all lovers. For the worth of the favor to the recipient would not   C
be as great, and the possibility of going unnoticed by others, if you wished to, would not be the same. But no harm ought to come from it; it should be of benefit to the pair of them. So I regard the things I've said as being sufficient, but if you want anything more and feel that it has been left out, just ask."

What's your impression of the speech, Socrates? Isn't it fantastically well done, especially in the choice of words?

SOCRATES Supernaturally so, my friend; I'm bowled over. And it's   D
all because of you that this happened to me, Phaedrus, because as I looked at you, it seemed to me that you were glowing with delight at the speech in the midst of reading it. And since I regard you as understanding more than I do about such things I followed along and in following I got swept up in the Bacchanalian frenzy under your divinely-inspired leadership.

PHAEDRUS Oh, so it's just a joke to you?

SOCRATES Does it seem to you that I'm joking and not being serious?

PHAEDRUS No more, Socrates; tell me truthfully, in the name of   E
Zeus, the god of friendship, do you believe there's anyone else among the Greeks who could say different things than these about the same subject, of higher quality and at greater length?

SOCRATES What? Is that the way the speech is supposed to be praised by you and me, as one in which the writer has said what he ought and not just because every word is clear and rounded-off and neatly polished? If that's the way it's supposed to be done, I'll just have to concede it for your sake, since it escaped my notice because of my ineptitude. I was only paying   235A
attention to the rhetorical side of it, and I thought that even Lysias himself wouldn't think that was adequate. In fact it

seemed to me, Phaedrus, though you may have something different to say, that he said the same things two or three times, as though he couldn't come up with any more to say about the same subject, or perhaps he just wasn't all that interested in such a thing. It appeared to me to be the performance of a beginner who was showing off his ability to say the same things in different ways and speak excellently in both versions.

B   PHAEDRUS You're talking nonsense, Socrates. That's exactly what the best thing is about the speech. He hasn't left out anything involved in the subject and worthy of being mentioned, so much so that no one could ever surpass the things he has said by making a greater number of points in a more worthy manner.

SOCRATES On that score I won't be able to agree with you any longer. If I go along with it just to satisfy you, the wise men and women of old[7] who have spoken and written about these things would refute me.

C   PHAEDRUS Who are they? And where have you heard anything better than this speech?

SOCRATES As to that, I couldn't say right now, but it's clear to me that I've heard some, possibly from the lovely Sappho or the wise Anacreon, or else some of the prose writers. And what's my evidence for saying this? It's a feeling I have welling up in my breast, my heaven-sent companion, that I'm filled with things I could say that are different from these and no worse. Now I know perfectly well that I haven't thought up any of that by myself, since I'm aware of my own ignorance, so I suppose the only explanation left is that by listening I've

D   been filled up like an empty vessel from waters flowing from other sources. But I'm such a dunce I've forgotten exactly who I heard these things from and how.

---

7. Socrates uses exactly the same rhetorical tactic in the *Meno* at 81A to introduce the myth of recollection, and Meno takes the bait in exactly the same way. By 275B of this dialogue, Phaedrus has learned to see through the trick.

PHAEDRUS Oh, you most magnanimous man, that's the most beautiful thing you could say! Don't tell me who you heard them from and how, not even if I insist on it; just do exactly as you say. Promise to say things different from and unrelated to those on the scroll, and say better ones and no fewer, and I promise you that I, like the nine archons,[8] will set up a golden full-sized statue at Delphi, and not only one of myself but one   E of you as well.

SOCRATES You are adorable, Phaedrus, and truly golden if you imagine I meant that Lysias had failed in every respect, and that I could say other things that differed from all of his. I don't suppose that could happen to even the most incompetent writer. For a start, on the subject of the speech, who do you think can argue that one ought to gratify a non-lover instead of a lover and pass over praising the good sense of the one and   236A blaming the foolishness of the other, which are surely inevitable points, and go on to say something else? I'd say things like that are permissible to the speaker and pardonable. In such cases it's not the conception but the execution that deserves to be praised; but with things that are not inevitable and are hard to come up with, praise is due for the conception as well as the execution.

PHAEDRUS I accept your point, since what you say seems quite fair. So here's what I'll do: I'll grant you the assumption that the non-lover is more sane than the lover, and then on the   B remaining points, if you say different things from those that Lysias has said, and more of them, and more worthily, take your stand at Olympia beside the hammered gold offering dedicated by the Cypselids.

---

8. Under Solon's constitution, the rulers of Athens swore an oath when they entered office to take no bribe, on penalty of paying restitution to the temple at Delphi with an offering worth the equivalent of the bribe; popular opinion seems to have transformed this into a statue of the offender himself, worth his own weight in gold.

SOCRATES Have you been taking me seriously, Phaedrus, for attacking your beloved, when I was just teasing you, and do you imagine that I'm really going to try to surpass his wisdom by saying something different and more varied?

PHAEDRUS My dear friend, this time you've got yourself into the same fix I was in before. Now more than anything you're required to speak to the best of your ability, so that we don't get forced into that tired old routine of the comedians who keep batting back each other's words. So be careful if you don't want to force me to say "Oh, Socrates! If I don't know Socrates, I've forgotten myself," and "he put on a show of being coy, as if he weren't just dying to speak." Just make up your mind that we're not leaving this spot until you speak and get those things off your chest that you said you had in there. We're alone in a deserted place, and I'm younger and stronger, so based on all that, "get my message" and don't have me resort to force when you can speak voluntarily instead.

SOCRATES But Phaedrus, you blessed soul, I'll make a fool of myself, compared to a good writer, if an ordinary man like me speaks off the cuff about the same things.

PHAEDRUS You know what? You'd better stop putting on this coy act with me, because I'm pretty sure I have something I can say to force you to speak.

SOCRATES Then please don't on any account say it.

PHAEDRUS Oh no, I'm speaking no matter what, and what I say will be on my oath. For I swear to you by—by whom, though; by which of the gods? Or would you rather I swore by this plane tree here? All right; if you do not deliver your speech to me in front of this very tree, I swear that I will never exhibit any other speech of anyone's to you or even tell you about one.

SOCRATES Oh, you rotten scoundrel! How well you've uncovered the way to force a man who loves speeches to do whatever you command!

PHAEDRUS Then why do you keep trying to wriggle out of it?

SOCRATES I won't any longer, after that oath you swore. How could I give up that sort of treat?

PHAEDRUS Then speak.   237A

SOCRATES Do you know what I'm going to do?

PHAEDRUS About what?

SOCRATES I'm going to speak with my cloak pulled up over my head, so I can race through the speech as quickly as possible and not be thrown off stride by glancing at you and feeling ashamed.

PHAEDRUS As long as you speak, you can do as you like about everything else.

SOCRATES Oh come ye mellifluous Muses, whether you bear this name for the tone of your song or from the melodious race of Ligurians,[9] join me in taking up the tale this most excellent man is forcing me to tell, to make his friend, who seemed wise to him before, seem more so now.   B

Once upon a time there was a boy, or rather a young man, quite a beautiful one, and he had very many lovers. Now a certain one of these was devious, and though he was no less in love than any of the others, he had persuaded the boy that he was not in love. And once when he was pressing his case, he actually tried to persuade him of this: that one ought to gratify a non-lover in preference to a lover. Here's what he said:

"For those who expect to make a good decision about anything, my boy, there is only one way to begin; one must know   C what the decision is about, or else one is bound to go wrong in every way. Most people aren't even aware that they're ignorant of the true nature of each thing. They assume that they do know it, and don't agree on terms at the beginning of their inquiry, and as they proceed they come to the result one could reasonably expect: they don't agree with themselves or with

9. After beginning his speech in a mock-poetic style, Socrates tosses in this pseudo-etymological wordplay connecting a standard epithet of the Muses (*ligeios*, "mellifluous") with the name of a tribe in northwest Italy.

each other. So in order that you and I may not suffer what we complain about in others, and since the proposition you and I have before us is whether one should preferably enter into friendship with someone who's in love or someone who's not, let us conduct our inquiry by setting down an agreed-

D   upon definition of love, both of what it is and what power it has, which we may keep an eye on and refer back to as we examine whether it provides benefit or harm. Now it is obvious to everyone that love is a desire, but we also know that even non-lovers desire beautiful things. By what, then, are we to distinguish the lover from the non-lover? We must take note of the fact that there is within each of us a pair of ruling and guiding forms which we follow wherever they lead: one is an innate desire for pleasures, the other an acquired opinion that strives for what is best. This pair within us are some-

E   times of one mind but they are sometimes in strife, and at times the one holds mastery, but at other times the other does. When opinion leads toward what is best by means of reason

238A   and holds mastery, the name of this mastery is self-control, but when desire drags us irrationally toward pleasures and rules within us, its rule is given the name unrestraint.[10] Now unrestraint goes by many names, because it has many parts and divisions, and of these forms, the one that happens to be preponderant gives its own name to the person who has the thing named, not a particularly beautiful or valuable thing to possess. If a desire for food holds mastery over reasoned judgment of what is best, and over the other desires, it is called gluttony

B   and gives that same name to the person who has it; if, in turn, the tyrannizing desire is for strong drink and leads the one who possesses it in that direction, it's clear what designation he gets, and it's correspondingly clear that the other names

10. The word translated "unrestraint" is *hubris*, used here in its fundamental sense of crossing all boundaries of decency. In the *Symposium* it is used in a wide range of meanings; see the note to 181C. In the *Phaedrus* most of its uses will suggest a horse that jumps out of its paddock.

akin to these, taken from the desires akin to these, will be applied in the appropriate manner according as one is predominant in each case. My object in saying all that has preceded is pretty obvious by this time, but what is stated explicitly is always clearer than what is not; so the desire which, in the absence of reason, holds mastery over an opinion that drives us toward what is right, and is itself directed toward the enjoy- C ment of beauty, and is forcibly reinforced (*errômenôs rhôstheisa*) by desires akin to itself and directed toward the beauty of bodies, and is victorious in its leadership, takes its name from its force (*rhômê*) and is called love (*erôs*)."[11]

Whew! My dear Phaedrus, does it seem to you, as it does to me, that I'm having a divinely-inspired experience?

PHAEDRUS Most assuredly, Socrates, you're in the grip of something beyond your usual eloquence.

SOCRATES Then listen to me in silence, for the place seems to have a genuine aura of divinity. So don't be surprised if, as I D proceed, I become possessed by the wood Nymphs from time to time. Even now the things I'm uttering are not so far from the ecstatic style of dithyrambs.

PHAEDRUS That is very true.

SOCRATES But it's you who are responsible for these things. Still, listen to the rest, for it may be possible to ward off the attack. That, however, is in the hands of a god; we must return to the boy in our speech.

"Now then, superb young man, the matter about which a decision needs to be made has been stated and defined, so keeping our eyes on that, let's speak about what remains, E namely any benefit or harm that will be likely to come from the lover or the non-lover to the one who gratifies them.

---

11. The etymological claim here is no more serious than that involving the Muses and the Ligurians, but the idea of love as an overpowering force may be found in writings of such poets as Sophocles (*Antigone* 781 and following) and Euripides (*Hippolytus* 525 and following).

"Someone who is ruled by desire and enslaved to pleasure will necessarily make his beloved as pleasing to himself as possible, and what is pleasant to someone of unsound mind is anything that does not resist him, while anything stronger or equal is hateful to him. So a lover will not willingly put up with a beloved boy who is his superior or his equal, but he always makes him feebler and inferior. But the ignorant is feebler than the wise, the cowardly feebler than the courageous, the incompetent speaker than the skilled rhetorician, and the slow-witted person than the quick-witted. When all these deficiencies of intelligence, and still more, arise and are implanted by nature in the beloved, the lover will necessarily be pleased and cultivate others, or else be deprived of his immediate pleasure. He will necessarily be jealous, and will prevent many other associations and benefits that would be most apt to make a man of the boy; this jealousy will be a source of great harm, the greatest harm being the prevention of that which would make the boy most wise. And this happens to be the divine pursuit of philosophy, from which a lover will necessarily keep his beloved boy far away, out of a great fear that he himself will be looked down upon. He will contrive other means of making the boy ignorant of everything, so he will have to look to his lover for everything, and as such he would be most pleasing to his lover but most detrimental to himself. So as far as the things having to do with intelligence are concerned, then, a man in the grip of love is by no means a profitable guardian or companion.

"The next thing one needs to examine is the condition of the body, and the means by which and manner in which someone who is driven to pursue the pleasant in preference to the good will take care of the person he has in his charge. And he will be seen seeking out someone who is soft and not sturdy, not raised in pure sunshine but in dense shade, accustomed not to manly exertion and dried sweat but to a delicate and unmanly way of life, adorned with artificial cosmetics for lack of a good complexion of his own, and devoted to all the other practices that go along with these, which are obvious and not worth going any further into. After summing it all up in a single main point, we may pass on to something else: it's the sort of body which, in war and all other occasions of great need, arouses confidence in his enemies and fear in his friends and even in his lovers themselves.

"That, then, may be left as clear, and the next point may be addressed, namely, what benefit or what harm the company and guardianship of a lover will bring us where possessions are concerned. And this much is perfectly clear to everyone, and especially to the lover, that what he would pray for above all is for his beloved to be bereft of the dearest and kindliest and most divine things that he possesses, because he would welcome seeing him deprived of his father and mother and relatives and friends, believing they would be hindrances and objectors to the relations he would find most pleasant with the boy. And he will think that someone who has wealth in the form of gold or any other property is not as easy to catch and, once caught, not as easy to control; as a result, it is entirely necessary that a lover will begrudge his beloved boy the possession of wealth and be happy about its loss. And therefore the lover's prayer would be that the boy continue to be unmarried, childless, and without a household of his own for the longest possible time, from a desire to have the enjoyment of his delights all to himself for the longest possible time.

"Now there are other evils, but some divine power has mixed a momentary pleasure in with most of them. A flatterer, for instance, is a dreadful beast and a great nuisance, but still nature has added an extra dash of pleasure to him that is not without its charm. One might also denounce a prostitute as harmful, along with many other such creatures and practices which might possibly be most pleasant, at least at the time. But a lover, in addition to being harmful to his beloved boy, is also the most disagreeable of all people to spend one's time with.

E

240A

B

C

The old saying has it that people flock to those of their own age—on the grounds, I imagine, that likeness in years leads to likeness in pleasures and turns similarity of tastes into friendship—yet even their companionship can get to be too much. And surely constraint of any kind is said by everyone to be oppressive, and the lover not only has the greatest dissimilarity to his beloved boy but holds him in the greatest constraint. An older man who associates with a younger one is unwilling to

D be left out of anything by day or night, but is under a necessity and plagued by the sting of it, which drives him on by giving him continual pleasures from seeing, hearing, and touching his beloved and perceiving him with every one of his senses, so much so that it is his pleasure to be his constant servant. But what consolation is that to the beloved? What pleasures could he give *him* to make that same length of time they spend together not come to the extremity of revulsion, as he looks at an aging face no longer in its prime, and at the other things

E that go along with that, which are not pleasant even to hear spoken of in words, to say nothing of being under the constant pressure of necessity to handle in fact. And what about the suspicious precautions with which he is guarded all the time against everybody, the unsuitable and extravagant praises he has to listen to, and likewise the taunts that are hard enough to bear when the lover is sober, but when he gets drunk and lets rip with a tedious and unrestrained flow of speech, are not just hard to bear but reprehensible?

"And as long as he's in love, he's harmful and unpleasant, but once his love has come to an end, he becomes undependable in the time that follows, for which he'd made many promises, along with his many oaths and entreaties, and barely

241A maintained during that time a relationship which was painful for the beloved to bear through hope of future good. But at the time when he's obliged to pay up, he's changed over to a different ruler and authority within himself, good sense and self-control in place of love and madness, having become, unbeknownst to the boy, a different person. The boy requests a favor from him in return for the ones he bestowed earlier, reminding him of the things that have been done and said, as if he were speaking with the same person, but from shame, the man cannot bring himself to admit that he's become someone else, but neither can he find any way of making good on his solemn declarations and promises from the earlier time, when irrationality ruled him, now that he's come to his senses and gained control of himself, fearing that by doing the same things and acting like that former self, he would become the same person again. Avoidance of those things ensues, the former lover has by default become a swindler, the shell has flipped over,[12] and he turns in the other direction and dashes off in flight. The boy is forced to chase after him with anger and curses, all because he didn't understand from the very start that one ought never to gratify a lover, someone who is necessarily out of his mind, but much rather a non-lover, a person who has good sense; otherwise he would necessarily be handing himself over to someone who's untrustworthy, hard to please, jealous, disagreeable, a detriment to his property and to the condition of his body, and by far the most detrimental of all to the cultivation of his soul, and there is nothing that is or ever will be more truly prized among human beings and gods than that. You must keep these things in mind, my boy, and realize that the friendship of a lover is not a matter of goodwill but is like the feeling he might have about food, for the sake of his own satisfaction.

Lovers are fond of boys all right, and wolves dote on lambs."

And that's that, Phaedrus. You won't hear me say any more beyond that; let my speech for you have its end right there.

---

12. In the oyster-shell game, a shell was tossed, and according as it landed with the dark or light side up, one group of children would chase the other.

PHAEDRUS But I thought it was only half done, and you'd say an equal number of things about the non-lover, how one ought to gratify him instead, stating all the good things he has on his side. So why are you stopping now, Socrates?

E   SOCRATES Didn't you notice, you blessed soul, that I'm already spouting epic verse and not even dithyrambs any more, and that's when I'm being critical? What do you imagine I'll come out with if I start lauding the other fellow? Don't you realize that I'll obviously become possessed by the wood Nymphs you exposed me to, knowing exactly what you were doing? So I say in one sentence that the good things that are the opposites of all the things we blamed the one fellow for apply to the other fellow. What need is there for a long speech? Enough has been said about the pair of them. That way my

242A   tale will get the treatment it deserves, and I'm crossing this stream and going away before I get forced into any more trouble by you.

PHAEDRUS Not yet, Socrates; not until the heat of the day passes. Don't you see that the sun is already almost standing at its zenith, at what's called "high noon"? Let's wait here and talk about what's been said, and leave as soon as it cools off.

SOCRATES You are more than human when it comes to speeches, Phaedrus; you're literally a wonder. I believe that out of all those living during your lifetime, no one has caused more

B   speeches to be given than you have, either by delivering them yourself or by putting pressure of one sort or another on others. I except Simmias the Theban from that statement, but you completely outclass everybody else. And now it seems that you'll be responsible for making me deliver another speech.

PHAEDRUS I won't take that as a declaration of war. But what's this I'm responsible for, and how?

SOCRATES My good man, at the moment I was about to cross the stream, my guardian spirit came, the one that usually comes

C   and gives me a sign; it always restrains me from something I'm about to do, and I seemed to hear a voice coming from it, forbidding me from leaving before I make atonement, as if I've committed some sin against the gods. Now I'm something of a prophet, not a very good one, but, like those who have little skill at reading and writing, just enough for my own needs. So I already understand the sin clearly. And you know, my friend, it's as though the soul even has a certain prophetic power of its own. Because all the time I was giving the speech something was bothering me, and I had some ill-defined misgivings that I might be doing what Ibycus calls "gaining honor among human beings at the price of offending the gods." But now I see where I went wrong.

D

PHAEDRUS What do you mean?

SOCRATES That was a dreadful speech you brought with you, Phaedrus, and a dreadful one you forced me to give.

PHAEDRUS How so?

SOCRATES It was simple-minded, and hardly short of blasphemous; what could be more dreadful than that?

PHAEDRUS Nothing, if what you say is true.

SOCRATES What? Don't you believe Love is the son of Aphrodite and is a god?

PHAEDRUS So it's said.

SOCRATES Not by Lysias, and not by your speech, the one that was spoken by you through my mouth as a result of your witchcraft. If Love is, as he most certainly is, a god or something divine, he could not be evil, but the pair of speeches that were just now given spoke of him as being such. So in that way both of them sinned against Love, and what's more, their simple-mindedness had this highly sophisticated air about it, because, while nothing they were saying was well-founded or true, they were solemnly pretending it was something profound, as if that might let them fool some poor excuses for human beings and get a high reputation among them. So I, my dear friend, am under an obligation to purify myself, and there is an ancient precedent for purification by those who have sinned in the telling of tales. Homer didn't know about

E

243A

it, but Stesichorus did, for when *he* lost his eyesight on account of his slander of Helen, he recognized the guilt that Homer was unaware of, and as a devotee of the Muses he immediately composed these lines:

> There is no truth to that story;
> You never set foot on those well-oared ships
B > Or came to the towers of Troy.

And as soon as he'd written the whole poem, called the *Recantation*, he recovered his eyesight on the spot. And in one respect I'll be wiser than they were; before I even suffer any consequences for my slander of Love, I'm going to try to atone for it with a recantation of my own, with my head bare and not covered up in shame as it was last time.

PHAEDRUS There is nothing you could say that would please me more than that, Socrates.

C SOCRATES That, my good Phaedrus, is because you realize how shameless it was to utter that pair of speeches, this last and the one read from the scroll. Imagine if some well-bred man of a gentle disposition, who was in love with someone else of the same sort, or had been loved by one at an earlier time, had happened to hear us saying that lovers flare up in violent fits of hostility over small matters and are jealous and harmful toward their beloved boys; don't you think he'd believe he was listening to people who were brought up among a bunch of sailors and had never seen a love fit for free society? He'd
D be far from agreeing with all our fault-finding about love, wouldn't he?

PHAEDRUS By Zeus, he just might, Socrates.

SOCRATES Well I'm ashamed of myself for his sake, and I'm afraid of Love himself, and so I want to wash away the bitter-tasting sound, as it were, with a fresh speech. And I advise Lysias to write as quickly as he can that, other things being equal, one ought to gratify a lover rather than a non-lover.

PHAEDRUS Rest assured; that's exactly how it will be. For when you have delivered your praise of the lover, there is every necessity that Lysias will be forced by me to write another speech on   E that same subject.

SOCRATES I believe that, as long as you are who you are.

PHAEDRUS Then speak up fearlessly.

SOCRATES But where's that boy I was talking to? He needs to hear this too; if it goes unheard, he might be too quick and gratify a non-lover.

PHAEDRUS He's right at your side, and he's always very close to you, whenever you want him.

SOCRATES Well then, beautiful boy, this is what you need to bear in mind: that former speech came from Phaedrus, son   244A of Pythocles, a man of Myrrhinus, but the one I'm about to give comes from Stesichorus, son of Euphemus, from Himera. What needs to be said goes as follows:

"There is no truth to the claim that, when a lover is present, one ought to gratify a non-lover instead, because the former is insane and the latter of sound mind. If madness were simply a bad thing, the statement would be perfectly fine. But the fact is, the greatest of good things come to us by way of madness, when it is bestowed as a gift of the gods. For the prophetess at Delphi and the priestesses at Dodona have con-   B ferred many beautiful blessings on Greece while they were mad, but few if any while in their right minds. And if we go on to speak of the Sibyl and all the others who have made oracular pronouncements under the spell of prophetic inspiration and have foretold many things to many people that set them on the right course for the future, we'd have to spend a long time stating things that are obvious to anyone. But it is worth citing as evidence the fact that the ancients who gave things their names did not regard madness as anything to be ashamed of or reproached for. Otherwise they would not have   C associated the very name 'mania' with the most beautiful of arts, the one that discerns the future, by calling it the manic art. They gave it that name because they considered madness to be something beautiful when it comes by divine dispensation, but people nowadays have the bad taste to insert the letter T, calling it the mantic art. And when the ancients gave a name to the investigation of the future made by sober-minded people from birds and other signs, since these people make use of thought to give human speculation (*oiêsis*) a grounding in insight (*nous*) and information (*historia*), they called it augury (*oionoïstikê*), which the newcomers nowadays call *oiônistikê*, to give it a solemn sound with the long O. So by the measure in which prophecy is more perfect and honored than augury, both the word than the word and the fact than the fact, the ancients bear witness that the madness which comes from a god is much more beautiful a thing than the sane self-control that has its source in human beings. Then too, in cases of the greatest illnesses and sufferings stemming from some ancient blood-guilt in certain families, madness has broken out with oracular powers and found relief for those in need of it by recourse to prayers and services to the gods, hitting upon purifications and rituals that make anyone who has it within himself, not only at that time but throughout succeeding time, safe and sound, a release discovered in the midst of his present afflictions by someone who is rightly mad and divinely possessed. And a third form of possession and madness comes from the Muses. It takes hold of a gentle and chaste soul and excites and inspires it to a frenzy of lyrical and other poetry that embellishes countless deeds of the ancients and educates the succeeding generations. But if anyone comes knocking at the doors of poetry without the madness inspired by the Muses, convinced that art alone will be sufficient to make him a poet, he will be a failure himself and the poetry of the sane man will be invisible in the radiance of that produced by madmen.

"All these beautiful accomplishments of madness that comes from the gods, and still more, I can recount to you. So let us not be frightened on that score; let no one get us excited over an argument meant to intimidate us into thinking that a reasonable friend ought to be preferred over an agitated one. Let him carry off the prize of victory only after he has demonstrated in addition that love is not sent from the gods as a benefit to the lover and the beloved. And we on our side must prove the opposite, that this sort of madness is bestowed upon   C us by the gods for our greatest happiness. And even if that proof is unconvincing to the clever, it will be convincing to the wise. First of all, then, we must grasp the truth about the nature of soul, both divine and human, by looking to the ways it acts and is acted upon, and the starting point for the proof is as follows.

"All soul is immortal; for what is perpetually in motion is immortal, and for anything that moves something else or is moved by something else the cessation of its motion is the cessation of its life. Now the only thing that never stops moving is something that moves itself, since it never departs from itself, and for all other things that move, this is the source and origin of their motion. But a source is ungenerated; for   D everything that is generated necessarily comes into being from a source, but that source itself cannot come from one, for if it were to come from a source, it would no longer be a source.[13] And since it is ungenerated it is also necessarily indestructible; for if a source were destroyed, it could not then come into being from anything and nothing could come into being from it, since all things must come into being from a source. Therefore, that which moves itself is the source of motion, and this is incapable of being destroyed or of coming into being, or else the whole heaven and all generation[14] would fall to a standstill   E and never have any way for motion to come into being again.

13. The translation here follows John Burnet's Oxford text.
14. Here the translation follows the text of W. H. Thompson and that in H. N. Fowler's Loeb edition.

But since that which is moved by itself has been shown to be immortal, no one need be ashamed to declare this very thing to be the true nature and definition of soul. For every body that has its source of motion outside it is soulless, but one that has it within itself and from itself is ensouled, since that is the nature of soul. But if this is the way things are, and that which itself moves itself is nothing other than soul, then by necessity the soul would be ungenerated and immortal.

246A

"This much about the immortality of the soul is sufficient, but about its form, the following needs to be said. A full account of all that it is would be a matter for a good and a lengthy explanation, but what it is like is possible for a human being to say in a briefer compass; let us, then, speak in the latter way. Let the power of the soul be imagined in the likeness of a composite of a team of winged horses and a charioteer. Now the horses and charioteers of the gods are all good themselves and of good stock, but those of others are mixed. And with us, first of all, the leader drives a pair of horses, and second, one of those horses is beautiful and good itself and from a thoroughbred stock, while the other is the opposite and comes of an opposite breed. So in our case, driving the chariot is necessarily difficult and uncomfortable. And now we must try to say why a living thing is called mortal or immortal. All soul has everything soulless in its care; soul traverses the whole heaven and takes on various forms at different times. When it is perfect and winged, it travels aloft and governs the whole cosmos, but a soul that has lost its feathers is carried along until it gets hold of something solid into which it can settle down, taking on an earthly body which, due to the power of the soul, seems to move itself, and the compound whole, a soul and body fitted together, is called a living thing and bears the name 'mortal.' It is not immortal by any reasonable account, but even though we have never seen or adequately conceived a god, we make up some sort of immortal living thing that has a body and has a soul, and has these united perpetually throughout

B

C

D

time. As for these matters, though, may they be and be spoken of in whatever manner might be pleasing to the god. Let us take up the reason for the loss of wings, which causes them to fall away from the soul.

"The natural capacity of a wing is to draw something weighty upward, raising it to the dwelling place of the race of the gods. Thus, of the things connected with the body, it partakes of the divine to the greatest extent. What is divine is beautiful, wise, good, and everything of that sort, and by these things most of all, the wings of the soul are nourished and grow, while their opposites, anything vile or evil, make them waste away and even destroy them. Now the great commander in the heavens, Zeus, drives a winged chariot and leads the procession, arranging and caring for all things, and an army of gods and spirits follows in his retinue, formed up in eleven divisions. Hestia is the only one of the gods who stays at home; all the rest of the twelve who have the status of ruling gods lead the way in their assigned posts. There are many blessed vistas and pathways within the heavens along which the happy race of gods goes round and round, each managing its own task, and any who is willing and able follows along, since jealousy can gain no foothold within the divine chorus. And when they go to a feast and a banquet, they go up the steep ascent to the pinnacle of the heavenly vault, where the chariots of the gods, with well-matched horses responsive to the reins, easily make their way, though the rest have difficulty. For the horse that has a share of badness is heavy, and unless one of the charioteers has done a beautiful job of training it, it sinks to the earth and drags the chariot down to the place where the hardest toil and struggle confront the soul. For those who are called immortals, when they reach the summit, pass on outside and stand on the broad back of heaven, and as they stand there, the celestial revolution carries them around and they behold the things outside the heavens.

E

247A

B

C

"No poet among us has ever yet sung of the place beyond the heavens, and none ever will sing of it worthily. But this is what it is like—for one must dare to tell the truth, especially when it is truth one is speaking about. This place, the province of true knowledge, is occupied by the kind of being that *is* in the fullest sense, the intangible being that has no color or shape and can be beheld only by the intellect, the steersman of the soul. And since the thinking power of a god is nourished by intellect and unadulterated knowledge, as is that of every soul that cares about receiving what is meant for it, it cherishes the opportunity for gazing upon being for a time and beholding truth, and it takes nourishment and joy from that until the circular motion carries it back to the same place. But in the course of its revolution it takes in view justice itself, it takes in view moderation, and it takes in view knowledge, not the knowledge that has any connection with becoming, and is in any way different when applied to different things among those which we now call beings, but the knowledge that is in and of the kind of being that *is* in the fullest sense. And when it has in the same manner beheld and feasted upon the rest of the beings that truly *are*, it sinks back into the interior of the heavens and goes home. And when it has come home, the charioteer halts his horses at the manger, throws in ambrosia, and gives them nectar to drink along with it.

"This is the life of gods, but among the other souls, the one that best follows and most resembles a god lifts the head of the charioteer into the outer region and is carried around with the revolution, but it is disturbed by the horses and can barely hold the beings in its view. Another sometimes rises and sometimes sinks, but because it keeps struggling with its horses, it sees some of the beings but not others. The rest, though they all yearn to follow the god upward, are unable to do so, and they are carried around under the surface, trampling on and jostling one another as some keep trying to get in front of others. So there is the utmost turmoil and con-

tentiousness and sweat, in which, as a result of a lack of skill
on the part of the charioteers, many horses become lame and
a lot of them have many feathers broken. All these souls go
away after considerable labor without having been initiated
into the sight of being, and after their departure they feed on
a diet of opinion. But the whole purpose of the great eagerness to see where the field of truth lies is that the appropriate grazing for the best part of the soul comes from the grassy   C
meadow that happens to be there, and the nature of the wing
by which the soul is lifted up is nourished by that. The ordi-
nance of Destiny is this: any soul that has become an adher-
ent of a god and seen any of the truths will be free of harm
until the next cycle of revolution, and if it can achieve this
perpetually, it will remain undamaged perpetually. But in
the case of a soul that is incapable of following and does not
see them, and by suffering some misfortune becomes filled
with and weighed down by forgetfulness and evil, once it has
become heavy it loses its feathers and falls to earth, then the
law is that this soul will not be implanted into the nature of   D
any beast in its first birth, but the soul that has seen the most
will come to be present in the birth of a man who is philosophic, or devoted to beauty or to any of the arts inspired by
the Muses, or is of an erotic nature; a soul of the second rank
will be born into a lawful king, or one who is warlike and fit
for command, one of the third rank into a politician or anyone good at managing a household or making money, fourth
a lover of hard work or athletic exercise, or someone who will
be concerned with the healing of the body, fifth someone who
leads the life of a prophet or conducts mystic rites; a soul of   E
the sixth rank will be fitted to a poet or someone who pursues one of the other imitative arts, one of the seventh rank
to a craftsman or farmer, eighth a sophist or demagogue, and
ninth a tyrant.

"Now at all these ranks, anyone who lives a just life takes
up a better fate and anyone who lives an unjust life, a worse

one. Each soul arrives at the same place it came from, but not
for ten thousand years, because it cannot gain its wings before
that time—not unless it has been a sincere philosopher or a
philosophic lover of boys. In these cases, if they've chosen that
life for three one-thousand-year periods in a row, they gain
their wings and depart in the three-thousandth year. The rest,
when they've come to the end of their first life, come up for
judgement, and once they have been judged, some go to places
of correction under the earth to pay their penalties, while others are lifted up by Justice to a place in the heavens to live
on in a manner worthy of the life they lived in the form of a
human being. But in the thousandth year, both sorts come
to a drawing of lots and a choice of a second life, and each
one chooses whatever life it wishes. At that time a human soul
may enter into the life of a beast, and one that was human
before may pass from a beast back into a human being. But a
soul that has never seen the truth may not take on this form,
because a human being has to be able to understand the spoken word by means of an intelligible look that comes from
many perceptions and is gathered into one by the reasoning
power. And this is a recollection of those things which our
soul once saw when it traveled in company with a god and
lifted its gaze beyond the things we now speak of as beings
and emerged into the realm of the things that truly are. And
so, quite justly, it is only the thinking of the philosopher that
recovers its wings, since he is always in the presence of those
things, as far as this is possible through memory, whose presence makes a god divine. And when a man makes correct
use of reminders of this sort, he is constantly being initiated
into the full mysteries and he alone becomes truly complete.[15]
But since he turns his back on the things human beings so

---

15. The words for "full," "mysteries," "be initiated," and "complete" all
share the same root, so the sentence contains the sequence *teleous aei teletas
teloumenos, teleos ontôs.*

busily pursue and becomes directed toward the divine, he is disparaged by the general run of people as being out of his mind, because those people are unaware of the fact that he is divinely inspired.

"Now then, the whole speech up to this point concerns the fourth kind of madness,[16] which, when someone sees the beauty here and recollects true beauty, and, becoming winged with restored wings and eager to wing his way aloft, cannot do so and gazes upward like a bird, ceasing to care about the things down here, causes him to incur the charge of being in a deranged condition. And it follows that, of all the ways of being possessed, this is the best and stems from the best sources, both for the one who has it and for anyone who comes to have a share in it, and that it is for his participation in this form of madness that someone in love with beautiful things is called a lover. For as has been said, every human soul has by its nature gazed upon the beings, or else it could not have come into this kind of living thing. But it is not easy for every soul to recollect those beings from the things here, not for those that saw the things there only briefly at that time, and not for the ones that, after falling, had the misfortune to be turned by some sort of associations toward injustice and into a state of forgetfulness of the holy things they saw then. Few are left in whom an adequate recollection is present, but these few, when they lay eyes on any likeness of the things there, are bowled over and can no longer control themselves, but they do not understand what they are experiencing because of the inadequacy of their perception. In these likenesses of justice and moderation and all the other things that are precious to souls, there is no radiance, but a few souls, when they come upon these images, see with difficulty through cloudy sense-organs the nature of their originals. But at that time it was possible to gaze upon a resplendent beauty, when with that happy chorus,

E

250A

B

16. The first three were described at 244A–245A.

ourselves following in Zeus's company and others with other gods, the souls beheld that blessed sight and spectacle and were initiated into the mysteries which tradition calls the most blessed of all and which we celebrated when we ourselves were still in a state of perfection and had not been exposed to all the evils that awaited us in the time to come, but were admitted into the highest of the rites and to visions perfect, simple, steadfast, and happy in pure light, pure ourselves and not entombed in this which we now carry around with us and call the body, bound to it the way an oyster is bound to its shell.

"Let this, then, be our tribute to memory, delivered at extended length now for its sake out of a yearning for the things of that earlier time. But we were speaking about beauty, and saying that, even among those beings, it shone out conspicuously, and since we came here we have apprehended it shining most clearly through the most distinct of our senses. For sight is the sharpest of the senses that reach us through the body, though wisdom is not seen by it—wisdom would arouse frightening passions of love if such a clear image of it were given to us as comes to sight—nor are the other lovable beings visible. Beauty alone is allotted that prerogative, and thus it is the most crystal-clear and love-inspiring of them all. But someone whose initiation is not recent, or who has been corrupted, is not swiftly transported to that place from this one toward beauty itself when he beholds its namesake here, and thus gazing upon it inspires no awe in him; instead, he gives himself up to pleasure, and tries to mount and spill his seed like a four-legged beast, and as he grows familiar with unrestraint he is not afraid or ashamed to pursue pleasure contrary to nature. But someone who was recently initiated and admitted to the sight of many things at that time, when he sees a godlike face or any bodily form that presents a good image of beauty, begins to shudder and some hint of those feelings of fear from that time creeps over him, and then as he gazes he feels a reverence as before a god, and if he were not afraid

C

D

E

251A

to get a reputation for being stark raving mad he would offer sacrifices to his beloved boy as if to a sacred effigy or a god. And as he keeps looking, a reaction from his shuddering sets in with an unusual sweating and heat, because he is warmed   B by the flowing stream of beauty he is taking in through his eyes, and by its moisture the growth of feathers is aroused. And as the warmth reaches the parts around the shoots, which for a long time had been closed up and hardened and prevented from sprouting, they soften, and with the flow of nourishment the shaft of each feather swells up and is stimulated to grow from the root all over the form of the soul, for it was originally all covered in feathers.

"Now in this condition, the whole soul is bubbling over   C and throbbing, and it is the same thing those who are teething go through when the teeth are just beginning to grow in and there is an itching and aching in the gums. The soul suffers in the same way when its feathers are beginning to sprout; it feels a bubbling and throbbing and tickling as the feathers grow. And then whenever it gazes upon the beauty of the boy, as it takes in the long stream of particles flowing from him (which is where longing gets its name),[17] it is moistened and warmed, and gains relief from its pain and a feeling of joy. But once the   D soul is separated from the beloved and dries out, the mouths of the passages from which the feathers germinate become thoroughly dried up and closed up and block off the sprouts of the feathers, and the sprouts that are shut up within with their longing throb like pulsing arteries as each one stings its own passage, so that the whole soul is pricked and prodded and in pain all over, but then again it fastens onto the memory of the beautiful boy and feels joy. The soul is distressed by this uncanny experience involving a mixture of both feelings,

17. The tortured etymology in the Greek purports to derive the word for "longing" (*himeros*) from *hienai merê*, with *rhein* possibly thrown in as well. At 255C, where this detail plays a crucial role, Socrates attributes the invention of the name to Zeus.

E and perplexed by its frenzy, and in its maddened condition it can neither sleep at night nor keep still anywhere by day, but its craving drives it to run wherever it thinks it might see the one who has such beauty. And when it sees him and is bathed in a flood of longing, the passages that were blocked open up, it gains a breathing space and a cessation of its stings and agonies, and that pleasure which it enjoys in those circumstances 252A is the sweetest of all. And for this reason, it does not willingly leave the beautiful one or care more about anyone than him. Instead, mothers, brothers, and all friends are forgotten, and if its wealth is lost through inattention, it counts that as next to nothing. It now has disdain for all the respectability and good manners it formerly prided itself on and is ready to act like a slave and to sleep wherever anyone will let it, so long as it can be closest to the one for whom it yearns. For in addition to B feeling awe for the one who has such beauty, it has found in him the only healer of its greatest sufferings. And to this experience, you beautiful boy to whom my speech is addressed, human beings give the name love, but when you hear what the gods call it, you'll laugh, because of your youth. But I believe some of the Homeridae recite two lines on Love from the apocryphal verses, one of which is full of poetic license[18] and not exceptionally metrical, and they chant them as follows:

C Mortals call him Eros, the god who soars on high,
  Immortals, Pteros, the wingsprouter he must be to fly.

You may give credence to those lines or not, but either way, that happens to be exactly what lovers experience and why.

"Now when one of the followers of Zeus is seized by the god named for his wings, it is able to bear the burden with

18. "Poetic license" here is *hubris*, in the sense of unrestraint or unruliness in which it is always used in this dialogue, as above in 238A and below beginning in 253E. The Homeridae were members of a clan on the island of Chios who claimed to be descendants of Homer.

greater dignity. But those who serve Ares and travel around with him, whenever they are captured by Love and think they have suffered any wrong at the hands of the beloved, are murderous and ready to sacrifice themselves and the beloved boy. And in the same way, each one who was a member of the troupe of each god lives its life honoring and, as far as it can, imitating that god, for as long as it is uncorrupted and still living out the first life into which it is born here on earth, and it behaves in that manner toward those it loves and everyone else it associates with. Thus, from among the beautiful, each one chooses its love in accord with its own inclination, and molds and adorns him like a sacred image, in order to revere and worship him, as though the beloved himself were his god. Those who adhere to Zeus, then, desire that the soul of the one they love might be Zeus-like, so they look for a nature that is philosophic and commanding, and once they've found him they love him and do everything with a view to forming his character in that way. If they have not embarked on this pursuit before, then they set out to learn anything they can from anyone at all, and to seek it out for themselves, and when they go looking to discover the nature of their god from within themselves, they find plenty of resources, because they are forced to gaze intently upon the god; by coming in contact with him through memory, they are inspired, and take on his character and way of life as far as it is possible for a human being to partake in the nature of a god, and since they give the credit for this to the beloved, they cherish him all the more. And if they draw the waters of their inspiration from Zeus, then like Bacchic revelers, they pour it out upon the soul of the beloved, making him as much like their god as possible. All those in turn who follow after Hera seek someone regal, and when they find him they do all those same things for him. And the followers of Apollo and of each of the gods in the same way go in quest of a boy of their own who has a nature in accord with the god, and once they've got hold of one, they lead him, as

D

E

253A

B

far as they can, into the conduct and semblance of that god, by imitating the god themselves and persuading and training the boy. There is no jealousy, no grudging[19] spitefulness in the way they treat the beloved boy; in order to lead him into the likeness of themselves and the god they honor, they spare no effort and no resources to make him that way as much as possible. Thus the whole-hearted desire of true lovers, and, if they accomplish what they are so eager for in the way I am describing, the rite of initiation that the object of this affection receives from the friend who is in the grip of the madness of love, becomes in this manner a beautiful thing and a source of happiness—if he is conquered, and the conquest of the one who is conquered takes place in the following manner.

"According to the three-part division we made of each soul at the beginning of this tale, two of them formed in the image of a pair of horses with the third form in the image of a charioteer, let these distinctions still be maintained by us now. We claim that one of the horses is good and the other is not, but we did not specify what constitutes the goodness of the good one or the badness of the bad, and this must now be stated. The one of the pair that holds the nobler position is upright in form, with muscles well-defined, its neck held high, and its nose slightly curved, and it is white in appearance and dark-eyed; it is a lover of honor combined with self-restraint and modesty, and a devoted disciple of true opinion; it needs no whip, but is driven by command with a mere word. But the other, in turn, is crooked, overweight, and lopsidedly put together, with a massive but short neck, a flattened nose, a dark skin, and grey and bloodshot eyes; it is a companion of unrestraint and swaggering, shaggy around the ears and deaf,

19. The word translated "grudging" is *aneleutheros*, tight-fisted as opposed to open-handed, or inhibited as opposed to free. It becomes an important word in 256A–257A in Socrates' final repudiation of his slander against divine madness.

and barely responds to a combination of whip and goads. Now when the charioteer sees the sight that arouses love, the whole soul is warmed by the sensation and filled with the tickling and pricking of yearning, and the horse that is obedient to the charioteer, constrained then as always by modesty, holds itself back from rushing at the beloved, but the other horse, no longer paying any attention to the goads and whip of the charioteer, is swept away and leaps with brute force, giving its yoke-mate and the charioteer all the trouble they can handle, and it presses them to go up to the beloved boy and make mention of the joy of sexual gratification. At first the other pair indignantly resist being forced to do dreadful and unlawful things, but at last, when there is no limit to the trouble, they go where they are being led, yielding and agreeing to do what is being insisted on. And so they get close enough to the beloved boy to behold the dazzling brightness of his face.

"But as the charioteer looks at him, his memory is carried back to the nature of beauty, and he sees it once again standing beside chastity upon a holy pedestal; and as his memory gazes in awe, the charioteer feels fear and falls backward, and this forces him to pull back so violently on the reins that both horses in the pair sink down on their haunches, the one willingly and without resisting, but the unruly one very unwillingly. And when the pair of them has gone farther away, the one horse from shame and amazement drenches the whole soul in sweat, but the other, once the pain it has from the bit and the fall subsides and it has barely recovered its breath, lets loose a torrent of angry abuse, hurling many reproaches at the charioteer and its yoke-mate for their cowardice and unmanliness in deserting their post and the agreement among them. And after it tries again to force its unwilling companions to move forward, it reluctantly complies with their entreaties to postpone that to another time. Then when the agreed-upon time arrives and both of them pretend to have forgotten, it

254A

B

C

D

reminds them, struggling and neighing and dragging them, and forces them to approach the beloved boy again with the same proposition; and when they've gotten close, it lowers its head, stretches out its tail, takes the bit between its teeth, and

E   pulls shamelessly. But the charioteer has the same experience he had before, and even more strongly; he falls back like a race driver at the finish-line, yanks the bit back forcibly out of the teeth of the unruly horse, bloodies the tongue and jaws of its foul mouth, and forces its legs and haunches down hard on the ground, inflicting pain on it. And when it suffers this same experience over and over, the bad horse gives up its unruliness, finally cowed into following the prudent guidance of the charioteer; now, when it sees the beautiful one it is overcome with fear. And so it turns out that, from that time on, the soul of

255A   the lover follows the beloved boy with reverence and awe.

"So now the beloved receives every kind of service, as if he were the equal of a god, from a lover who is not pretending but truly experiencing love, and the beloved himself is by his nature disposed toward friendship with the one doing the service; as a result, even if he has previously been misled by his schoolmates or any others who call it a shameful thing to consort with a lover, and for that reason has kept his distance from his lover, as time goes on his age and destiny eventu-

B   ally lead him to accept him into his company. For surely it cannot be within the allotted order of things for bad to be a friend to bad, or for good not to be a friend to good. And once he has accepted the lover and welcomed his conversation and his company, the goodwill apparent in the lover from up close astonishes the beloved, and he sees clearly that all the rest of his friends and relatives put together have no modicum of friendship at all to offer him in comparison to the friend who is divinely inspired. And as the lover continues to keep company with him and get close to him, with all the touch-

C   ing that involves during exercises and other intimate occasions, then eventually the fountain of that stream to which

Zeus gave the name 'longing' when he fell in love with Ganymede[20] pours over the lover in abundance, and while some of it enters him, some, when he has all he can hold, overflows outside him; and just as a wind or an echo is sent bouncing back off smooth, hard surfaces to the place it came from, so too does the stream of beauty come back to the beautiful one through the eyes, the natural opening to the soul, and having arrived there it stimulates the regrowth of its feathers, waters $\quad$ D their passageways, excites the sprouting of wings, and fills the soul of the beloved with love. And so the beloved is in love, but has no idea who he is in love with; he doesn't know what has happened to him and can't even describe it, like someone feeling the effects of an eye disease caught from someone else and unable to say what caused it. He is seeing himself in his lover as if in a mirror, but doesn't realize it. And when his lover is present, he ceases from his pain in the same way as the lover, but when, in turn, his lover is absent, he yearns in the same way he is yearned for; he has a returned love in love's $\quad$ E image, but what he calls it and believes it to be is not love but friendship. He feels a desire almost exactly like that of his lover, though not as strong, to see him, touch him, kiss him, and lie down beside him, and as one would expect, he quickly after that does those things. And when they are lying together, the undisciplined horse in the lover's soul has something to say to the charioteer, and claims he deserves a little satisfaction in return for his many troubles; the one in the boy's soul has $\quad$ 256A nothing to say, but is bursting with passion and at a loss to say why, and he embraces and kisses the lover, in appreciation for someone so overwhelmingly considerate. And when they are lying together, there is nothing the lover could ask for that he,

20. More than forty human women were seduced or raped by Zeus, according to various myths. Ganymede was the one boy any of those myths claimed was the object of his lust. In Plato's *Laws* (636C–D), the Athenian Stranger says that the people of Crete invented that story to legitimize a practice the Stranger himself does not approve of.

for his part, would refuse to do to gratify him, but his yoke-mate, along with the charioteer, resists these things with modesty and reason.

"Now if the better powers of the mind prevail and guide them to a composed way of living and to philosophy, they lead a blessed and harmonious life here on earth, being their own masters with orderly characters, suppressing that which admits badness into the soul and setting free that which admits virtue. And when this life is ended, they have become winged and unburdened, victors in one of the three falls in the wrestling match that is truly Olympic,[21] and neither human prudence nor divine madness is capable of providing a human being with a greater good than that. But if they lead a coarser way of life, one without philosophy but ruled by a love of honor, then most likely in a state of drunkenness or at some other careless moment, their two undisciplined beasts will pair up, catch their souls off-guard, get them together in the same place, grab the opportunity that most people would consider the most blissful, and do the deed. And once it's been done, they go on doing it afterward, though not frequently, since doing so does not seem like a good idea to the whole mind. These two men are friends, though less so than that other pair, and they spend their lives with each other, both while the love lasts and after they've gotten beyond it, believing that they've given and received the greatest pledges of fidelity, and that it would not be permissible ever to break them and get onto bad terms. And though they end up without wings, they depart from the body feeling the beginning of an impulse to grow wings, so that it is no small prize they carry off from the madness of love. For it is ordained that those who have already begun their journey under the heavens will not go again into the darkness and the journey under the earth, but will be happy as they live a life in brightness, traveling side-by-side,

21. See 249A.

and thanks to their love, they will, when the time comes, be identically winged.

"These blessings, my boy, so great and so divine, will be bestowed upon you by the friendship that comes from a lover, but the relationship that arises with a non-lover, which is diluted with mortal prudence and doled out with mortal stinginess, will give birth in the soul of the beloved to the inhibition that is praised by most people as virtue. That will cause   257A it to drift, dim-witted, for nine thousand years upon the earth and beneath it."

And this recantation is offered up to you, dear Love, as your due, the best and most beautiful speech in our power, especially in some poetic phrasing I was constrained to use for Phaedrus's sake. Grant me forgiveness for my earlier words and look with favor on these; be gracious and merciful unto me and do not in anger take away or impair that art of love you have bestowed upon me, but allow me to be even more admired by the beautiful than I am now. And if Phaedrus   B and I spoke any harsh word about you in our previous discourse, put the blame on Lysias, the father of that speech, stop him from giving such speeches, and turn him, as his brother Polemarchus has been turned, to philosophy, so that this lover of his here may no longer vacillate the way he does now but devote his life single-mindedly to love through philosophic discussions.

PHAEDRUS I join you, Socrates, in praying that these things may come to pass, if that is indeed best for us. But I've been in a   C state of wonder at your speech all along, at how much more beautifully-crafted you made it than your previous one. So I'm afraid Lysias may appear second-rate, if he's even willing to put another one on display up against it. Just the other day, in fact, you wonderful man, one of the politicians was criticizing him and inveighing against this very thing, and all through his invective he kept calling him a speechwriter. So perhaps his love of honor might prevent him from writing for us.

SOCRATES That's a laugh, young fellow, and your judgment about
your companion is way off-target if you think he's so apt to
shy away from a little prattle. You're probably even assuming
that the man making the invective against him was sincere in
his criticism.

PHAEDRUS He certainly seemed to be, Socrates, and you yourself
are surely aware that the men who wield the greatest power
and are held in the highest respect in our cities are ashamed
to write speeches and leave behind any writings of their own,
because they're afraid of the reputation that might follow them
if they're called sophists.

SOCRATES You've missed the point, Phaedrus; it's just sour grapes.[22]
And sour grapes aside, don't you realize that the politicians
with the highest opinions of themselves are the ones who love
speechwriting and leaving writings behind the most, so much
so that in every case they write in a notation at the beginning
of those who approve of them?

PHAEDRUS What do you mean by that? I'm not understanding.

SOCRATES Don't you understand that the beginning of a political
man's writing has the approval written first?

PHAEDRUS How's that?

SOCRATES Surely the writer says "It was resolved by the senate" or
"by the people" or both, and "so-and-so proposed," naming
and lauding himself very solemnly, and then after that he goes
on to show off his own wisdom for their approval, sometimes
composing a very long document. Does such a thing seem to
you to be anything other than a written speech?

PHAEDRUS Not to me.

SOCRATES And if this motion carries, its author steps out of the
auditorium gleeful, but if it's made null and void, and he gets

---

22. The Greek has "it's just a sweet elbow, so-called from the long bend
in the Nile." The passage has attracted much comment over the millennia, but
not much illumination, and the explanatory portion is most likely a gloss that
crept into the text.

thwarted in his speechwriting and found unworthy of being a writer, he and his companions are grief-stricken.

PHAEDRUS Very much so.

SOCRATES Which makes it clear, at any rate, that they don't consider themselves too good for that practice, but are in fact full of admiration for it.

PHAEDRUS Quite so.

SOCRATES And what happens when a rhetorician or a king is good enough at his task to gain the power of a Lycurgus, a Solon, C or a Darius, and to achieve immortality as a speechwriter in a city? Doesn't he consider himself the equal of a god in his own lifetime, and don't succeeding generations regard him in that same light as they gaze in awe upon his writings?

PHAEDRUS Very much so.

SOCRATES So do you suppose anyone like that, whoever he may be and however antagonistic to Lysias, could revile him just for being a writer?

PHAEDRUS It's not likely, based on what you're saying, since it seems he'd be reviling what he himself desires.

SOCRATES Therefore this is obvious to everyone, that writing D speeches, in and of itself, is no disgrace.

PHAEDRUS How could it be?

SOCRATES Instead, I assume, what's disgraceful is speaking and writing disgracefully and badly rather than well.

PHAEDRUS That's clear.

SOCRATES So what is the way of writing that makes it good or not? Do we need to examine Lysias about that, Phaedrus, and anyone else who has ever written or ever will write anything, whether it's a political document or a private work, either in meter as a poet or without meter as a layman?

PHAEDRUS You're asking if we need to? What other purpose is E there for living, if I may say so, than the pursuit of such pleasures? It's certainly not for the sake of those one can't enjoy without previous pain, which is how it is with pretty much all the pleasures involving the body, and is the reason they're rightly referred to as fit for slaves.

SOCRATES Well, we have the time, it seems. And besides, it seems to me that in this stifling heat, the cicadas up above our heads
259A are looking down at us as they sing and talk to one another. If they should see the pair of us behaving the way most people do in the middle of the day, not having a conversation but dozing and caught up in the spell of their song through inertia of our mental powers, they would rightly laugh at us, thinking some slaves had come to their hideaway to spend the noontime lazing around the stream like sheep. But if they see us talking and sailing right past them as if they were Sirens and
B we were immune to their song, they might be so impressed they'd give us the reward the gods put in their keeping to give to humans.

PHAEDRUS What's this they have in their keeping? I don't think I've ever heard of it.

SOCRATES It's unseemly for a man who's devoted to the Muses not to have heard of such things. The story is that these cicadas were once human beings, at a time before the birth of the Muses, but after the Muses were born and song made its appearance in the world, some humans at the time were so
C bowled over with the pleasure of it that they just kept singing and neglected food and drink, and didn't even notice that they were dying off. After that the race of cicadas arose from them, and was given this reward from the Muses, that they were born needing no nourishment at all, but straight from birth would sing, without food or drink, until they died, and afterward go to the Muses to report who among those on earth honors each of them. To Terpsichore, they report those who have honored
D her in dances, and make them more beloved to her, to Erato, those who have honored her in matters pertaining to love, and likewise to the rest, according to the form of honor paid to each. To Calliope, the eldest Muse, and Urania, the next-eldest after her, they report those who spend their lives in phi-

losophy and honor the music presided over by these Muses, who, more than all the others, are concerned with speeches divine and human, and who utter the most beautiful strains. For many reasons, then, one ought to talk about something during the middle of the day and not sleep.

PHAEDRUS Yes, one ought to talk.

SOCRATES Well then, the thing we were just now proposing to   E examine, the principle that makes one way of speaking and writing good and another bad, is what ought to be explored.

PHAEDRUS Clearly.

SOCRATES And if things are going to be said effectively and beautifully, mustn't a knowledge of the truth about the things he's going to talk about be present in the mind of the speaker?

PHAEDRUS As to that, my dear Socrates, I've heard it put this way: that it's not necessary for someone who's going to be a rhetori-   260A cian to understand what justice truly is, but what would seem just to a multitude of people who'll be passing judgment, or what is truly good or beautiful but what things would seem that way, since persuasion is based on these things and not on truth.

SOCRATES And whatever wise men utter, Phaedrus, is "not a word to be lightly brushed aside,"[23] but one ought to examine it in case there's anything in what they say. So the thing that was just said ought not to be passed over.

PHAEDRUS You're right about that.

SOCRATES So let's examine it this way.

PHAEDRUS What way?

SOCRATES If I were persuading you to get yourself a horse to fight   B the enemy, and we were both ignorant of what a horse is, but I happened to know this much about you, that Phaedrus believes a horse is the domesticated animal that has the longest ears . . .

PHAEDRUS That would be ridiculous, Socrates.

23. *Iliad* II, 361.

SOCRATES Not yet, but it would be when I go on persuading you into it in all seriousness, composing a speech in praise of the donkey, but calling it a horse and saying that it's an animal worth any price to have around the house and on military ser-

C vice, useful as a mount to fight from and able to carry equipment, and serviceable in many other ways.

PHAEDRUS That would be totally ridiculous.

SOCRATES But isn't it better to be ridiculous and a friend than to be clever and an enemy instead of a friend?

PHAEDRUS Apparently.

SOCRATES So then, when a rhetorician who is ignorant of what's good and evil takes on the task of persuading a city that's in the same condition, not about some figment of a donkey that he pays tribute to under the impression that it's a horse, but about something evil under the impression that it's good, after he's studied the opinions of the multitude, and he persuades them to do evil things instead of good ones, what sort

D of crop do you think that rhetorician will harvest from sowing those seeds?

PHAEDRUS Not a very adequate one.

SOCRATES Well then, good fellow, have we disparaged the art of speeches more crudely[24] than we should? It might perhaps reply, "What nonsense are you spouting, you absurd people? I don't force anyone to learn how to speak without knowing the truth, but if my advice is anything to go by, it's to take me up after acquiring that. What I boast of is this: that without me, knowing how things are won't make anyone any more capable of artful persuasion."

E PHAEDRUS And will it be speaking justly in saying that?

SOCRATES I'd say so, if the arguments coming up against it corroborate that it *is* an art. Because I have this feeling I'm hearing some arguments rising up and declaring that it's a fraud,

---

24. This is the comparative of the word used in 229E for the "rustic" (*agroikos*) wisdom that challenges myths for not being literally true.

and not an art at all but an artless routine.[25] A genuine art of speaking that doesn't hold to the truth does not exist and never could, or so a Spartan might say.

PHAEDRUS Those arguments are needed, Socrates; bring them   261A
here and examine what they say and how they say it.

SOCRATES Come ye, then, noble creatures, and persuade Phaedrus, who has beautiful progeny of his own, that if he does not engage in philosophy enough, he will never be competent enough to speak about anything. And let Phaedrus answer.

PHAEDRUS Ask, noble creatures.

SOCRATES Wouldn't rhetoric as a whole be some sort of art of moving souls by means of speeches, not only in law courts and all other public gatherings but in private ones as well, the same thing in small matters as in great ones, no more to be esteemed   B
for its right use when it comes up on serious concerns than on trivial ones? Or how have you heard these things spoken of?

PHAEDRUS Not that way, by Zeus! Absolutely not. It's mostly about how lawsuits are argued and written by art, but also how speeches in the assembly are given. I haven't heard anything beyond that.

SOCRATES What? You've only heard of the textbooks on speeches by Nestor and Odysseus, that the two of them wrote in their spare time at Troy, but you're unacquainted with those by Palamedes?

PHAEDRUS I am, by Zeus, and with Nestor's too, unless you're   C
passing off a certain Gorgias as Nestor and a certain Thrasymachus or Theodorus as Odysseus.

SOCRATES Maybe so, but let's leave them out of it, and you tell me what it is that the litigants in law courts are doing. Aren't they making opposing speeches? Or what shall we say?

PHAEDRUS That very thing.

---

25. Such arguments can be found in the *Gorgias*, where Socrates says at 465A that rhetoric does not deserve to be considered an artful pursuit because it can give no rational account of how it achieves its results. The reference to Spartans may reflect their taste for unpretentious opinions delivered in pithy sayings.

SOCRATES About what's just and unjust?

PHAEDRUS Yes.

SOCRATES Then someone who does that by art will make the
D   same thing appear to the same people at one time as just, but
        then whenever he pleases, as unjust?

PHAEDRUS Certainly.

SOCRATES And in the legislative assembly he'll make the same
        things seem good to the city at one time and the opposite at
        another?

PHAEDRUS That's it.

SOCRATES And don't we know that when the Palamedes from Elea
        speaks by art he can make the same things appear to his hear-
        ers as like and unlike, one and many, at rest and in motion?[26]

PHAEDRUS Very much so.

SOCRATES So then the art of making opposing speeches is not
E   only for law courts and the legislative assembly, but it would
        apparently be one and the same art, assuming it is an art, for
        all kinds of speaking, and by means of it someone will be able
        to make every possible thing resemble every possible thing,
        and bring to light the fact that someone else is surreptitiously
        making such a resemblance.

PHAEDRUS What do you mean by such a thing?

SOCRATES I expect it will become evident to us if we examine it in
        the following way. Does more deception occur in things that
        differ much or little?

262A   PHAEDRUS In those that differ little.

SOCRATES And you'll get away with turning something into its
        opposite better by changing it in small steps than in big ones.

PHAEDRUS How could it be otherwise?

SOCRATES Therefore, someone who's going to deceive another
        person and not be deceived himself needs to distinguish accu-
        rately the likeness and unlikeness among the things there are.

PHAEDRUS Necessarily so.

---

26. The reference is to Zeno. See Plato's *Parmenides* 127D–130A.

SOCRATES Well then, if he doesn't know the truth about some particular thing, will he be capable of discerning a resemblance, small or large, between that unknown thing and other things?

PHAEDRUS That would be impossible.   B

SOCRATES Hence, when people are deceived and hold opinions contrary to the way things are, it's clear that this problem has crept in by way of some sort of resemblances.

PHAEDRUS That certainly does happen.

SOCRATES Then is there any artful way for someone to mislead others by small steps through resemblances so as to lead them on each occasion from the way something is to its opposite, or to avoid this himself, if he is unacquainted with what each of the beings is?

PHAEDRUS None whatsoever.

SOCRATES Therefore, my friend, an "art of speeches" that's pro-   C
vided to us by someone who doesn't know the truth but is chasing down opinions will be something laughable and not an art at all.

PHAEDRUS It's looking that way.

SOCRATES Then do you want to take a look in the speech of Lysias that you're carrying and in the ones we gave for some of the things we're claiming are artless and artful?

PHAEDRUS More than anything, because we're talking abstractly now, and don't have enough examples.

SOCRATES Well, by a stroke of luck, it seems, the pair of speeches that were delivered contain an example of how someone who   D
knows the truth can mislead his listeners by playing games with words. And I credit this to the gods who haunt this place,[27] Phaedrus, and perhaps those prophets of the Muses who are singing above our heads might be the ones who inspired us with this gift, because I certainly don't have any part in any art of speaking.

PHAEDRUS If you say so; just make clear what you're saying.

---

27. At 236E, Phaedrus picked out the plane tree, *platonos*, as a local god.

SOCRATES Come then; read me the beginning of Lysias's speech.

E PHAEDRUS "You know my situation, and you've heard what I think is the advantageous way for these things to be handled. And I don't think I deserve to be denied this request of mine just because I don't happen to be in love with you. Lovers have second thoughts at the time when . . ."

SOCRATES Stop there. Where this goes astray and what makes it artless need to be said, right?

269A PHAEDRUS Yes.

SOCRATES And this much is clear to everyone, isn't it, that we are of one mind about some things of this sort but at odds about others?

PHAEDRUS I think I understand what you're saying, but put it more clearly.

SOCRATES When someone says the word "iron" or "silver," don't we all have the same thing in mind?

PHAEDRUS Surely.

SOCRATES But what if he says "just" or "good"? Don't we go our separate ways and disagree with one another and even with ourselves?

PHAEDRUS Very much so.

B SOCRATES Then we're in harmony on some matters but not on others.

PHAEDRUS Just so.

SOCRATES Then in which case are we more easily fooled, and on which matters does rhetoric have greater power?

PHAEDRUS Obviously on those we have shifting opinions about.

SOCRATES Then anyone who's in quest of an art of rhetoric must first make a methodical division and get hold of some distinctive look that belongs to each of the two kinds, that on which most people necessarily shift their opinions and that on which they don't.

C PHAEDRUS Anyone who gets hold of that would have a beautiful sight for his mind's eye to behold, Socrates.

SOCRATES Next, I imagine, when a particular case comes up, he must not let it go unnoticed but must sharply discern which class the thing he's going to speak about happens to belong in.

PHAEDRUS Certainly.

SOCRATES Then what about love? Would we claim that it's one of the things on which opinions shift or on which they don't?

PHAEDRUS One of those on which opinions shift, presumably. Otherwise, do you think it would give you an opening to say the things you said just now, that it is harmful to the beloved and the lover, and then again that it happens to be the greatest of all goods?

SOCRATES That's an excellent point. But tell me this, because I D was so carried away that I've completely forgotten whether I gave a definition of love at the beginning of my speech.

PHAEDRUS By Zeus, you did, and inconceivably forcefully.

SOCRATES Aha, then you're saying the nymphs, daughters of Achelous, and Pan, son of Hermes, are that much more artful with speeches than Lysias, son of Cephalus. Or am I completely wrong? Did Lysias, at the beginning of his discussion of love, require us to think of love as one definite thing of his E own choosing, and then finish by organizing everything in the rest of his speech in relation to that? Do you want us to read the beginning of it again?

PHAEDRUS If you think that's a good idea, but what you're looking for is not there.

SOCRATES Recite it anyway, so I can hear his own words.

PHAEDRUS "You know my situation, and you've heard what I think is the advantageous way for these things to be handled. And I don't think I deserve to be denied this request of mine 264A just because I don't happen to be in love with you. Lovers have second thoughts about the benefits they confer at the time when their desires come to an end."

SOCRATES He certainly seems to be a long way from doing what we're looking for, when he doesn't even start from the beginning but from the end, and then tries to swim upstream through his speech by doing the backstroke; he starts from things the lover would finish up by saying to his beloved boy. Or am I getting it all wrong, Phaedrus, dear heart?

B PHAEDRUS What he's making the speech about is certainly a conclusion, Socrates.

SOCRATES And what about the rest? Don't the things in the speech seem to be tossed out in a heap? Or does it appear that the thing said second needs to be placed second for some compelling reason, any more than any of the other things he says? It seemed to me, as one who knows nothing about it, that whatever came to him was said by the writer, though not ungracefully. Do you know of any necessity of speechwriting technique that led him to place these things one after another in just this order?

C PHAEDRUS You're being too kind if you think I'm competent to discern his reasons with such precision.

SOCRATES But I imagine you'd assent to this, that every speech ought to be organized like a living thing, having a body of its own, so that it's not lacking a head or feet but has a middle and extremities, composed to fit with one another and with the whole.

PHAEDRUS How could anyone not assent to that?

SOCRATES Take a good look at your friend's speech, then, to see whether it's like that or not, and you'll find that it's no different from the epitaph that some people say is inscribed on the tomb of Midas the Phrygian.

D PHAEDRUS What's that, and what's wrong with it?

SOCRATES It goes like this:

A bronze maiden I am, and I lie on Midas's tomb.
As long as water flows and tall trees send out leaves,
Remaining in this place on his much-lamented grave,
I'll proclaim to passers-by that Midas is buried here.

I assume you notice that it makes no difference which line of   E
it is said first or last.

PHAEDRUS You're mocking our speech, Socrates.

SOCRATES Then so as not to irritate you, let's leave that speech
aside, even though it does seem to me to contain an abundance of examples it might be helpful for one to look at, but
not exactly for the sake of trying to imitate them, and let's
move on to the other speeches. For they had something in
them worth looking at, I think, for those who want to inquire
about speeches.

PHAEDRUS What sort of thing do you mean?   265A

SOCRATES Presumably they were a pair of opposites, since they
claimed on the one side that a lover, on the other that a non-
lover, ought to be gratified.

PHAEDRUS And quite manfully.

SOCRATES I thought you were about to tell the truth and say
"madly." In any case, that's the very thing I was thinking of.
We did claim that love is a kind of madness, didn't we?

PHAEDRUS Yes.

SOCRATES And also that there are two forms of madness, one
coming from human disorders and the other from a divine
disturbance of customary habits.

PHAEDRUS Quite so.   B

SOCRATES And we divided the divine madness into four parts,
belonging to four gods, attributing prophetic inspiration to
Apollo, mystic rites to Dionysus, poetic inspiration to the
Muses, and a fourth form, the madness of love that we claimed
is the best form, to Aphrodite and Eros. And we made an
image, I know not how, of the experience of love, and perhaps
touched on some truth, though we were probably led astray
at some points; and once we had mixed together an account
that was not wholly unconvincing, we warbled some sort of   C
mythic hymn, in modest and pious tones, to your lord and
mine, Phaedrus, to Love, the guardian of beautiful boys.

PHAEDRUS And to me, at least, it was by no means unpleasant to listen to.

SOCRATES Then let's take up the following point from this example, how the speech was able to switch from blame to praise.

PHAEDRUS What do you mean by that?

SOCRATES It appears to me that in other respects the speech was really childish play, but in the course of these things that were said pretty much at random, there was a pair of forms, and if one could get an artful grasp of how they work, that would not be displeasing at all.

D

PHAEDRUS What are they?

SOCRATES One is the bringing together of a scattered multiplicity into a single comprehensive view, so that one may demarcate and make evident the particular idea about which one wants to give an explanation on any occasion. That's what was done about love just now—what it is was demarcated, and whether it was stated well or badly, at least this enabled the speech to be made with clarity and internal consistency.

PHAEDRUS And what is the other form you're speaking of, Socrates?

E

SOCRATES Being able to divide things up into kinds again at their natural joints without trying to fracture any part after the manner of an unskilled butcher. And that's what was just done in our pair of speeches; the irrational element in our thinking was taken in common as one particular form, and in the same way the body, though one, is naturally double with parts on the left and right called by the same names, so too our pair of speeches considered the form of derangement as one thing by nature within us, and one speech cut off the part on the left and kept cutting this repeatedly without stopping until finding within these divisions what one might call a sort of left-handed love which it quite properly reproached, while the other speech led us into the divisions of madness on the right-hand side and found a type of love that has the same name as that one but is divine, and presented this to view and praised it as the cause of the greatest good to us.

266A

B

PHAEDRUS What you say is completely true.

SOCRATES Now I myself, Phaedrus, am a lover of these divisions and collections, because they make it possible for me to speak and think, and whenever I believe anyone else is capable of insight into what is one or many by nature, I pursue that person as if I were following "in the footsteps of a god."[28] And god alone knows whether the name I give to those who are able to do this is right or not, but up to this time I've referred to them as skilled at dialectic.[29] But tell me what one ought to call people who've learned the things that come from the mouths of you and Lysias these days; is this that art of speeches by which Thrasymachus, and the others who use it, have become expert at speaking themselves, and make others experts too if they come to them bearing gifts fit for a king?

C

PHAEDRUS They are kingly men, but they don't have the kind of knowledge you're asking about. You seem to me to be right in calling that form of knowledge dialectical skill, but it seems to me that rhetoric is still eluding us.

SOCRATES What do you mean? Can there be any worthy thing that's left out of these skills but is still included in art? By all means it must not be disdained by you and me, but what this remaining part of rhetoric is must be stated.

D

PHAEDRUS There are a great many such things, Socrates, in the books that have been written about the art of speeches.

SOCRATES It's good of you to remind me. I believe that an introduction needs to be delivered first at the beginning of the speech; these are the things you mean—the refinements of the art—is that right?

28. See *Odyssey* V, 193.

29. In the *Meno*, at 75D, Socrates explains dialectic as the way of asking and answering questions suited to friends having a conversation, and says that it seeks not merely to find a truthful answer but to derive it from things the other person already accepts as true. Dialectic is treated in the dialogues as opposed to rhetoric in general, which starts with a conclusion and seeks persuasion, and to *hê antilogikê technê* in particular, by which either a rhetorician or a philosopher like Zeno seeks to construct a refutation of an opposing argument.

E   PHAEDRUS Yes.

SOCRATES And second a narrative of the facts with testimony attached to it, third the evidence, fourth the likelihoods, and I believe the man from Byzantium, that exceptionally subtle wordsmith, speaks of corroboration and secondary corroboration.

PHAEDRUS Do you mean the worthy Theodorus?[30]

267A   SOCRATES Who else? And he tells how rebuttal and re-rebuttal need to be done in both accusation and defense. And shouldn't we bring the highly esteemed Evenus the Parian front and center, the man who was the first to invent subliminal suggestion and oblique praise—and some say he also delivered oblique censure in verse to make it memorable—a wise man indeed. But Tisias and Gorgias we'll leave to their slumbers, the men who looked upon likelihoods as deserving of higher honor than truths, who make small things appear great and great things appear small through the sheer power of speech,

B   who state novelties in old-fashioned ways and the opposites in newfangled ones, and who invented pithiness of speech as well as immense length on all subjects. Prodicus laughed once when I told him that and said that he was the only one to discover what the art of speeches demands: that they be neither long nor short but just right.

PHAEDRUS Prodicus, you are superlatively wise!

SOCRATES And shouldn't we mention Hippias? I suspect that visitor of ours from Elis would cast his vote along with Prodicus.

PHAEDRUS Why not?

SOCRATES And what do we say about Polus and his Muse-oreum

C   of phrases, with its duplicative technique, gnomic style, and

---

30. Gorgias, Thrasymachus, and Theodorus were alluded to and dismissed from the discussion at 261C. Here they are brought back in along with some half-dozen other teachers of rhetoric, only to be dismissed again along with anyone who may have dealt with "minor" and superficial points of rhetorical composition. Throughout the dialogue, the only rhetoricians mentioned by Socrates with any seriousness or respect are Pericles (269E–270A) and Isocrates (278E–279B).

figurative language, plus the vocabulary Licymnius presented him with for manufacturing eloquence?

PHAEDRUS And weren't there some similar Protagorean terms, Socrates?

SOCRATES Oh yes, my boy, optimal wording and many other lovely things. But for tear-jerking speeches that wring out pity for old age and poverty, it's plain to me that the champion of the art is the mighty Chalcedonian,[31] and he was also a formidable man at stirring up anger in a crowd and then soothing   D the angry mob with incantatory words—he said so himself. And when it came to slandering or refuting slanders, any which way, he was the best. There seems to be common agreement among them all about the ending of speeches, though some give it the name recapitulation and others call it something else.

PHAEDRUS You mean reminding the listeners in a summary at the end of each point that's been spoken of?

SOCRATES That's what I mean, and anything else you might have to add about the art of speeches.

PHAEDRUS Just minor things, not worth mentioning.

SOCRATES Let's let the minor things go, then, but let's look at   268A these others under a stronger light to see what power of art they have, and when.

PHAEDRUS A very forceful power, Socrates, in popular assemblies at any rate.

SOCRATES So they do, my remarkable[32] friend, but you take a look and see if it seems to you the way it does to me, that the fabric of them has holes in it.

PHAEDRUS Just show me.

---

31. Thrasymachus, who is depicted at his fiercest in Bk. I of the *Republic*.

32. Socrates calls Phaedrus *daimonië*, a common form of address but literally a reference to a semi-divine spirit. Since the word "forceful" that Phaedrus has just used recalls the definition of love in this dialogue at 238C, a reader may be reminded of Diotima's identification of love as a *daimôn* in the *Symposium* in 202E.

SOCRATES All right, tell me: if someone came to your friend Eryximachus or his father Acumenus and said "I know various
B treatments to apply to bodies, to make them warm if I want
to or cool them off, and make them vomit if that seems like
a good idea to me, or else have a bowel movement, and all
sorts of other things like that, and since I know them I consider myself to be a physician and to be able to make someone
else one by passing on the knowledge of these things," what do
you imagine they'd say when they heard that?

PHAEDRUS What else but ask if he also knew who to do each of
those things to, and when, and how much?

SOCRATES And what if he said, "Not at all, but I think the per-
C son who learned these things from me is capable of doing the
things you ask about on his own."

PHAEDRUS I imagine they'd say the fellow was crazy, and after
hearing about something out of a book somewhere, or running across some drugs, he thought that made him a physician
when he had no understanding of the art.

SOCRATES And what if someone came to Sophocles or Euripides and said that he knew how to compose very long speeches
about a small matter and very short ones about a great matter,
and tear-jerking ones whenever he wanted to, or just the oppo-
D site, frightening and threating ones and everything of the sort,
and he thought that by teaching these things he could trans-
mit the ability to compose tragedies?

PHAEDRUS I imagine they'd get a laugh out of it too, Socrates,
if anyone assumed that a tragedy was anything else than an
arrangement of these things that combined them in a way that
was fitting to one another and the whole.

SOCRATES But I don't imagine they'd insult him rudely; rather,
they'd act the way a musician would if he met up with a man
who thought he was skilled at harmony because he happened
E to know how he could produce the highest and lowest notes
on a string. He wouldn't make some brutal remark like "you
worthless good-for-nothing, you're demented." Being a musi-

cal sort, he'd speak more gently and say, "You fine fellow, it *is* necessary for anyone who's going to be skilled at harmony to know these things too, but that doesn't prevent someone with your level of knowledge from not understanding harmony in the least. You know the things that it's necessary to learn as preliminaries to harmony, but not the things that constitute harmony itself."

PHAEDRUS Quite right.

SOCRATES So Sophocles would say the man was trotting out 269A before them the preliminaries to tragedy but not the things that constitute tragedy, and Acumenus, the preliminaries to medical art but not the things that constitute medical art.

PHAEDRUS Absolutely.

SOCRATES And what do we suppose the dulcet-voiced Adrastus, or even Pericles, would say if they heard the things we were just going over, those gorgeous refinements of the art such as pithiness of speech and figurative language and all the other things we said needed to be passed under a light and examined? Would they, like you and me in our boorishness, be so B harsh as to speak some rude word about those who have written and taught these things as the art of rhetoric? No, they, being wiser than we, would scold the pair of us and say, "Phaedrus and Socrates, there's no need to be so abrasive; you should make allowances if some people who don't know how to be dialectical have been unable to define what rhetoric is, and because of this misfortune have assumed that when they possessed the things one needs to learn as preliminaries to the art they had discovered rhetoric itself, and believed that when C they had taught these preliminaries to others they had taught them the totality of rhetoric, and that it is no trouble at all to speak persuasively with these various techniques and compose a whole speech, so that their students themselves need to provide these things on their own in their speeches."

PHAEDRUS Yes, Socrates, it certainly is likely that the part of the art that these men teach as rhetoric is something of that sort,

and you seem to me to be telling the truth. But as for the true
D   art of rhetoric and persuasion, how and from whom can one
obtain that?

SOCRATES The ability to become a consummate competitive
speaker is probably, and perhaps necessarily, like anything
else, Phaedrus. If you have it in you by nature to be rhetorical, you will be a notable rhetorician once you've added knowledge and practice, but if you're deficient in any of these, you'll
be imperfect in that respect. But for as much of it as is consti-
tuted by art, it seems obvious to me that the method by which
it is obtained is not the way of Lysias and Thrasymachus.

PHAEDRUS What is, then?

E   SOCRATES Most likely, my excellent friend, Pericles became the
most accomplished of all men at the art of rhetoric.

PHAEDRUS Why's that?

SOCRATES All great attainments in the arts need to be grounded
270A   in extensive and lofty discussions about nature, for these studies foster an elevation of the mind and an ability to carry a
task through to completion in every direction, qualities that
seem to be transferable to the practice of the arts. And Pericles, in addition to being naturally talented, did acquire these,
because I believe it was through meeting up with Anaxagoras,[33] who was just that sort of person, that he became filled
with lofty thoughts and carried his thinking up to the nature
of intellect and the lack of it, subjects on which Anaxagoras
discoursed at length, and he drew from these studies what was
beneficial to the art of speeches.

PHAEDRUS What do you mean by that?

B   SOCRATES Well, presumably the art of rhetoric works the same
way as the medical art.

PHAEDRUS How so?

SOCRATES In both of them it's necessary to analyze a nature, that

---

33. Anaxagoras taught that intellect (*nous*) governs all things and is responsible for all motion and multiplicity.

of the body in the one and that of the soul in the other, if you're going to go about it not merely by experience and routine but by art, so as to instill health and vigor in the one case by administering medicines and diet, and to impart in the other the persuasion and virtue you intend by means of speeches and customary practices.

PHAEDRUS It probably is that way, Socrates.

SOCRATES And do you suppose it's possible to grasp the nature   C
of a soul in any way worth mentioning without grasping its nature as a whole?

PHAEDRUS If one is to give any credence to Hippocrates the Asclepiad, one cannot even grasp the nature of body without that method.

SOCRATES And he's quite right about that, my friend. But the authority of Hippocrates notwithstanding, we ought to put his opinion to the test of reason to see if it's in harmony with it.

PHAEDRUS I'd say so.

SOCRATES Then consider what Hippocrates and true reason say about nature. And isn't the following the way one needs to think about the nature of anything whatever? First, if we wish   D
to be artful about anything and to be able to make others artful, we must think about whether it is simple or multiple in form; then, if it's simple we must consider its power, what natural capacity it has for acting on what, or for being acted upon by what, and if it has more than one form we must spell them out and, just with the single form, see in each case what it has a nature to do itself to what, or to be acted upon by what.

PHAEDRUS Likely so, Socrates.

SOCRATES At any rate, a procedure omitting these steps would appear to be like the progress of a blind person. But surely   E
no one at all who proceeds by art ought to bear a likeness to a blind or deaf person, so it's obvious that anyone who gives speeches to anyone by art will make evident precisely what the inherent nature is of that to which those speeches are addressed, and that will undoubtedly be the soul.

PHAEDRUS What else?

271A SOCRATES Then all his effort is intent upon the soul, since it is within the soul that he is striving to produce persuasion. Isn't that so?

PHAEDRUS Yes.

SOCRATES And therefore it is clear that Thrasymachus and any-one else who is serious about transmitting the art of rhetoric will first write with complete precision about the soul and make us see whether it is by nature one and uniform or has a form that is manifold like that of the body, for we claim this is what makes its nature evident.

PHAEDRUS Absolutely.

SOCRATES And secondly, he will write about what it does by nature to what, or how it is acted upon by what.

PHAEDRUS What else?

B SOCRATES And thirdly, he will make a systematic classification of the kinds of speeches and kinds of soul and go through all the causes of the effects produced upon the latter, adapting each kind of speech to each kind of soul and explaining which souls are for what reason necessarily persuaded by which speeches and which are not persuaded.

PHAEDRUS It does seem that would be the most beautiful way to go about it, at any rate.

SOCRATES There's no other way, my friend, that any explanation or speech will ever be spoken or written by art, none whatso-
C ever apart from this. Those who write the "arts of speeches" you've listened to nowadays are charlatans who hide the things they know perfectly well about the soul. So until they start speaking and writing by this procedure, we can't be persuaded that they write by art.

PHAEDRUS What procedure?

SOCRATES It's not easy to state the wording itself, but I'm willing to describe the way one needs to write if he's going to be as artful as possible about it.

PHAEDRUS Describe it, then.

SOCRATES Since the power of speech happens to be to move souls, it's necessary for anyone who's going to be a rhetorician to   D know how many forms of soul there are. There are this many and that many, of this and that sort, on account of which some people become one way and others another. Once these distinctions have been made in this way, there are also this or that many forms of speeches, each of a certain kind. And people of certain kinds are easily persuaded into certain beliefs by speeches of certain kinds for a particular reason, while people of other kinds are hard to persuade by them. After one has gained a sufficient grasp of these distinctions, one must observe them as they are present and carried out in actions, and be able   E to keep accurate track of them with his senses, or else he will be no better off for the things he understood when he was listening to speeches. But when he is sufficiently able to tell what sort of person is persuaded by what sort of speeches, and is able to distinguish someone he comes across and indicate to himself that this is the person and this is the nature about which those   272A speeches were speaking, now present before him in fact, and he must now bring to bear upon him the particular speeches in the particular manner that will bring about persuasion into particular beliefs, by the time he has all this and has also grasped the occasions on which one ought to speak or refrain from speaking, and has discerned the opportune and inopportune moments for pithy speech and tear-jerking speech and hyperbole and all the forms of speeches he has learned, then and not before will the art be beautifully and perfectly brought to completion. But if anyone is lacking any of this in his speak-   B ing or teaching or writing and still claims to be speaking by art, the one who disbelieves him wins the argument. "Now then, Phaedrus and Socrates," perhaps the author of our treatise might say, "is that how it seems to you? Is there not some other way of describing the art of speeches that one ought to accept?"

PHAEDRUS It's surely impossible to describe it any other way, Socrates, but it seems to be no small task.

SOCRATES You're telling the truth. So for that reason, we'd better examine all our statements, turning them up and down to
C see if any easier and briefer road to the art appears, so that one
doesn't needlessly go off down a long and rough one when he
has a short and smooth one available. So if you've heard anything helpful anywhere, from Lysias or anyone else, try to recollect it and tell it.

PHAEDRUS If trying would help, I'd be able to, but at the moment
I have nothing of the sort to say.

SOCRATES Then do you want me to tell you something I've heard
said by people who concern themselves with these things?

PHAEDRUS Why not?

SOCRATES It is said, at any rate, Phaedrus, that it's only fair to
speak as an advocate for the wolf.

D PHAEDRUS Please do so, then.

SOCRATES Well, these people say there's no need to be so solemn about these things and trace them back up such a long
and roundabout route. For as we said at the beginning of this
discussion, someone who's going to be a competent rhetorician has absolutely no need to get involved in the truth about
what things are just or good, or what people are of that sort
by either nature or upbringing. In the law courts, no one has
any concern in the least for the truth about these matters, but
E only for what is plausible. And since that is what is likely, the
one who's going to speak by art needs to fix his attention on
that. There are times when one ought not even to mention
the facts themselves, if they're not things that were likely to be
done, but only speak of what was likely, whether in accusation
or defense. On all occasions, the likely thing is what a speaker
needs to pursue, and on many he ought to say goodbye to the
273A truth, because when that happens through a whole speech, it
furnishes the whole art.

PHAEDRUS What you've just gone over, Socrates, is exactly what
those people say who profess to be artful about speeches. And
I'm reminded that we gave this sort of thing short shrift in the

earlier part of our conversation, but it does seem that it's given great importance by those who deal with these things.

SOCRATES Surely you've made a careful perusal of Tisias's own words, so let Tisias tell us whether he says that what's likely is anything other than the way something seems to most people.   B

PHAEDRUS What else?

SOCRATES And as a consequence of this astute and artful discovery of his, it seems, he wrote that if a man who is weak but brave beats up a strong coward and steals his cloak or something like that, and is brought into court, neither one of them should tell the truth; the coward should claim that the brave man didn't beat him up alone, and the latter should offer proof that the two of them were alone and then rely on that standard   C
line, "How could someone my size even lay a hand on someone like him?" The other man won't admit his own cowardice, and if he tries some other lie, he'll probably hand his adversary an opening for a refutation. And for other cases there are some such rules for speaking by art, aren't there, Phaedrus?

PHAEDRUS Certainly.

SOCRATES Oh my goodness, how cleverly it seems Tisias has unearthed a secret art—either he or whoever else it happens to have been and whatever name he has the happiness to be called by. But, my friend, should we tell him or not . . .

PHAEDRUS Tell him what?   D

SOCRATES This: "As a matter of fact, Tisias, some time ago, before you joined us, we happened to be saying that this likelihood is produced in most people precisely because of a likeness to truth. And we were just going over how in every situation, the person who knows what's true is in the most beautiful position to know how to discover likenesses to it. So if you have anything different to say about the art of speeches, we'll listen, but if not, we'll be persuaded by the things we've already gone over, that someone who can't distinguish and reckon up the   E
natures of his listeners and isn't able to divide beings according to their kinds and comprehend each particular thing one

by one under a single form will never be artful with speeches
to the extent possible for a human being. And these are capac-
ities he will never acquire without a lot of study and applica-
tion, labor which no sensible person ought to undergo for the
sake of speaking and acting before human beings, but to be
able, to the height of his power in all matters, to say what is
gratifying to the gods and act in a manner gratifying to them.
For those who are wiser than we, Tisias, say that anyone with
any sense ought not to devote himself to gratifying his fel-
low-slaves, except as a side-effect, but his good and high-born
masters. So don't be surprised if the way around to the goal is
long, for it has to be travelled for the sake of great ends and
not the ones you're imagining, though these too, if one wishes,
will be attained in the most beautiful way by those means, as
the argument says."

274A

PHAEDRUS That seems to me most beautifully spoken, Socrates, if
only one were able to do that.

SOCRATES But it's a beautiful thing even to make the attempt for
beautiful ends and take whatever comes of it.

B

PHAEDRUS Very much so.

SOCRATES Well then, let that be enough about art and artlessness
in speeches.

PHAEDRUS Quite so.

SOCRATES But what about appropriateness and inappropriateness
in writing, and what makes it turn out well or inappropriately?
That still remains, doesn't it?

PHAEDRUS Yes.

SOCRATES Well do you know the best way to gratify the god in
acting or speaking about rhetoric?

PHAEDRUS Not at all. Do you?

C

SOCRATES I can tell you something I heard from our ancestors,
but only they know the truth of it. But if we could discover
that for ourselves, would we care any more about human
opinions?

PHAEDRUS There's a ridiculous question! Just tell what you claim you've heard.

SOCRATES I've heard that at Naucratis in Egypt there was one of the ancient gods of that country, whose sacred bird was called the ibis, and the name of this divinity himself was Theuth. And he was the first to invent counting and calculating and geometry and astronomy, and also checkers and dice, and most importantly, letters. Now at that time, the king of all Egypt was the god Thamus, who was at the great city of the upper region which the Greeks call Egyptian Thebes, and they call the god Ammon. And when Theuth came to the king to display his arts, and said they should be passed on to the rest of the Egyptians, Thamus asked him what benefit each of them conferred, and Theuth went through them. And Thamus said whatever seemed good or bad to him, and praised the one sort and blamed the other. And it is said that Thamus declared many things to Theuth, both for and against each art, which would be a long story to go through, but when he came to the letters, Theuth said, "This piece of learning, your majesty, will make the Egyptians wiser and better at remembering, for I have discovered a formula for memory and wisdom." But the king said, "Most artful Theuth, someone may be capable of generating the things of art while someone else is capable of judging what portions of harm and benefit they have in them for those who are going to use them. And now you, being the father of letters, because of your partiality, are claiming a power for them that is just the opposite of what they have. For this invention will produce in souls a forgetfulness of the things they have learned, through a lack of practice with memory. Because of a trust in writing, that consists of external marks alien to themselves, they will not recollect on their own from out of themselves. So it is a formula not for memory but for reminding that you have invented. You are providing those who learn it not with a true but a seeming wisdom, for having

D

E

275A

become well-informed, thanks to you, without being taught,
B   they will seem to be full of knowledge when they are for the
most part ignorant, and they will be hard to be around, being
wise in their own conceit but not wise."

PHAEDRUS You easily make up stories about Egyptians or anyone
else you want, Socrates.

SOCRATES My friend, people used to say that the first prophetic
utterances were the words of the oak tree in the sacred pre-
cinct of Zeus at Dodona. The people of those days, who wer-
en't wise like you youngsters, were content in their simplicity
C   to listen to an oak or a rock just as long as it spoke the truth.
But perhaps it makes a difference to you who the speaker
is and where he comes from, since you do not look only to
whether that's the way things are or not.

PHAEDRUS You're right to rebuke me, and in the case of letters, it
seems to me that things are exactly as the Theban says.

SOCRATES So anyone who imagines he's left behind an art in writing, and also anyone who takes it up imagining that anything
clear and certain could come from writing, would be full of a
great simple-mindedness, and actually ignorant of Ammon's
prophecy in imagining that written words are anything more
D   than a reminder to someone who knows the things that are
written about.

PHAEDRUS Quite correct.

SOCRATES For there's this strange thing about writing, Phaedrus,
that's truly similar to painting, because the figures in a painting stand there like living beings, but if you ask them a question, they maintain a profound silence. And written words
are the same; you might think they were speaking with some
understanding, but if you ask a question because you want
to learn something about what they're saying, they just keep
E   pointing to the same single thing endlessly. And once it's written down, every speech makes the rounds everywhere, among
those who understand and those who have no interest alike,
and it doesn't know whom it ought to speak to or not. And

when it's misconstrued and unjustly criticized it always needs help from its father, since it has no power of its own to defend or help itself.

PHAEDRUS These points too are quite correctly taken.

SOCRATES And what about this? Can we see another kind of speech, a legitimate brother of this kind both in the way it's born and the extent to which it's naturally better and more powerful from birth?   276A

PHAEDRUS What's that, and what do you mean by the way it's born?

SOCRATES Speech which is written with knowledge in the soul of someone who understands it and which is capable of defending itself and knows to whom it ought to speak or keep silent.

PHAEDRUS You mean the living and breathing speech of someone who has knowledge, of which written speech may justly be said to be an imitation.

SOCRATES Absolutely. Now tell me this. If a farmer has any sense,   B and has some seeds he cares about and wants them to bear fruit, would he, as a serious matter, plant them in the summer in little shallow pots[34] and be delighted to see beautiful sprouts come up in eight days, or would he do that only as amusement for a holiday, if he did it at all? When he was being serious, wouldn't he observe the precepts of the art of farming and plant his seeds in suitable ground, and then be content when everything he planted reached its full growth in the eighth month?

PHAEDRUS He would undoubtedly do it that latter way, Socrates,   C as a serious matter, and the other way, as you say, for the opposite reason.

SOCRATES And are we going to claim that someone who has knowledge about what is just and beautiful and good has less sense about his own seeds than a farmer?

---

34. Literally, "in gardens of Adonis." These were potted plants meant to sprout quickly and quickly wither and die, to be buried at an annual festival in tribute to Adonis, a human lover of Aphrodite who died young.

PHAEDRUS He least of all.

SOCRATES Therefore, he's not seriously going to write them in water, that black inky water that transmits through a pen words incapable of helping themselves in an argument and incapable of teaching the truth in an adequate way.

PHAEDRUS That doesn't seem likely.

D   SOCRATES Because it's not. What seems likely is that he'd plant those word-gardens for amusement, and write, when he does write, to store up reminders for himself for the time when he comes into the forgetfulness of old age, and for anyone who travels that same track, and he will take pleasure in seeing them putting forth tender shoots. While others pursue other amusements, indulging themselves at drinking parties and all the other things that are closely akin to these, he will most likely divert himself with the recreations I'm speaking of, rather than those.

E   PHAEDRUS You're speaking of a thoroughly beautiful amusement as against a low-grade kind, Socrates, that of someone capable of finding amusement in speeches, who concocts tales about justice and the other things you're talking about.

SOCRATES And so it is, dear Phaedrus, but I think a serious effort about them is much more beautiful, when someone who makes use of the dialectical art takes a suitable soul and sows and plants in it words with knowledge in them, potent to help

277A   themselves and the one who planted them, and these words are not fruitless but contain a seed that engenders others in other soils which have the potency to make this process deathless for all time, and to make the one who possesses them happy to the greatest extent possible for a human being.

PHAEDRUS This that you tell of is indeed much more beautiful still.

SOCRATES And now that we've agreed about these things, Phaedrus, we are able to render judgment on those others.

PHAEDRUS What others?

SOCRATES The ones we wanted to look into, on account of which

we got to this point, so we could evaluate the criticism of Lysias
for being a writer of speeches, and also about the speeches   B
themselves, which ones were written by art and which without
art. It seems to me that what is and is not within the realm of
art has been made tolerably clear.

PHAEDRUS I did have that impression, but remind me again how
that went.

SOCRATES One needs to know the truth about the various things
one speaks or writes about, and be able to define each in its
own right, and having defined them, know how to divide
them up into kinds until he reaches indivisible classes; one
needs also to have a clear grasp in that same manner of the
nature of the soul and discover the form that corresponds to   C
each nature, and design and arrange the speech accordingly,
providing a motley soul with motley speeches that hit all the
notes and a simple one with simple speeches. Until then he
will not be competent in the art to the full extent that the
class of speeches can naturally be manipulated, either to teach
something or to persuade anyone about something, as our
whole preceding discussion has revealed to us.

PHAEDRUS That is absolutely the way it came to light.

SOCRATES And what about whether it's noble or base to deliver   D
and write speeches, and what circumstances would make it
justly be said to be a disgrace or not? Didn't we make it clear
in the things we said a little while ago that . . .

PHAEDRUS What things?

SOCRATES That if Lysias or anyone else ever did or ever will write
anything in private or by proposing laws in public as the
author of a political document, thinking it had anything of
great reliability and clarity in it, in that case it is a disgrace
to the writer, whether anyone calls it that or not. For awake
or asleep, to be ignorant of the things that are just and unjust   E
and bad and good cannot escape being a reason for disgrace in
truth, even if the whole crowd applauds it.

PHAEDRUS Not at all.

SOCRATES But one who thinks there is inevitably much that is playful in the written word, on any topic, and that no speech that's ever been written in meter or in prose is worthy of high esteem, not even if it's declaimed with all the skill of the reciters of Homer, for the sake of persuasion without examination and instruction, but that the truth of it is that the best of them are reminders of things one already knows, and who thinks that only in words concerning the just and the beautiful and the good that are taught and spoken for the sake of learning and truly written in the soul is there anything clear and complete and worthy of serious esteem, and that speeches of this kind ought to be spoken of as his own legitimate offspring, first of all the word within himself, if it is in him as his own discovery, and then any descendants and brothers of that one that may have sprung up in a worthy manner in other souls of other people, and who bids goodbye to words of the other sort—well then, Phaedrus, he is likely to be the sort of man you and I would pray that you and I might become.

PHAEDRUS What you say is absolutely what I want and what I would pray for.

SOCRATES Then let this be enough playing about speeches for us. You go and tell Lysias that the two of us came down to the stream sacred to the Nymphs and shrine of the Muses and listened to words that commanded us to speak to Lysias and anyone else who composes speeches, and to Homer and anyone else who has composed poetry with or without song, and thirdly to Solon and whoever has written those documents involved in political discourse that he calls laws. If they have composed these things with knowledge of the truth about what is in them, being able to defend them if an argument comes up about what they've written, and with the capacity to demonstrate by their own words that written words are trifling things, then such people ought not to be referred to by a title based on these writings but by those based on the things they take seriously.

PHAEDRUS What titles do you give out to them?

278A

B

C

D

SOCRATES To call them wise seems to me to be overdoing it, Phaedrus, and appropriate only for a god, but either philosophic or something of that sort fits better and is less pretentious.

PHAEDRUS There's nothing unreasonable about it.

SOCRATES But as for the person who has nothing more valuable than the things he's composed or written, and spends his time tweaking them this way and that, sticking in words in place   E of one another or taking them out, would it not be just if you called him a poet or speechwriter or lawmaker?

PHAEDRUS What else?

SOCRATES Then tell that to your friend.

PHAEDRUS And how about you? What will you do? For your friend shouldn't be overlooked.

SOCRATES Who's that?

PHAEDRUS The beautiful Isocrates.[35] What will be your message to him, and what shall we call him?

SOCRATES Isocrates is still young, Phaedrus, but I'm willing to state a prophecy I can make about him.   279A

PHAEDRUS What is it?

SOCRATES It seems to me that his natural gifts are superior to those displayed in the speeches of Lysias, and that they're mingled with a nobler character. Thus it wouldn't come as a surprise to me at all if, as he advances in age, assuming he keeps putting his efforts into the same sorts of speeches he writes now, he excels those who have ever turned their hands to speeches more than if they were children, and if those sorts of works are not satisfying to him, some motivation of a more divine kind may lead him to even greater things. Because, my friend, something of a philosophic nature is present in the   B man's thinking. These, then, are the messages I'm carrying away from the gods of this place to my beloved boy Isocrates, while you carry those others to Lysias, who is yours.

35. Isocrates wrote speeches that combined a style he learned from Gorgias with ideas he picked up by associating with Socrates.

PHAEDRUS So it will be. But let's go, now that the stifling heat has become milder.

SOCRATES Isn't it fitting for someone going away to offer a prayer to the local gods?

PHAEDRUS What else?

SOCRATES Dear Pan, and all the other gods of this place, grant that I may become beautiful inwardly, and that all my outward possessions may be favorable to what is inside. May I regard him who is wise as wealthy, and may I possess as much gold as no one but a self-restrained person could bear or carry.

C

   Do we have need of anything more, Phaedrus? To me that prayer seems to be just right.

PHAEDRUS Let me join in this prayer, for the things of friends are shared in common.

SOCRATES Let's go.